History of Australia

A Captivating Guide to Australian History, Starting from the Aborigines Through the Dutch East India Company, James Cook, and World War II to the Present

Free Bonus from Captivating History (Available for a Limited time)

Hi History Lovers!

Now you have a chance to join our exclusive history list so you can get your first history ebook for free as well as discounts and a potential to get more history books for free! Simply visit the link below to join.

Captivatinghistory.com/ebook

Also, make sure to follow us on Facebook, Twitter and Youtube by searching for Captivating History.

Contents

Introduction

Millions of years ago, Australia was home to dinosaurs, and prehistoric animals roamed the lands. Thousands of years ago, the first people set foot in Australia. They were ancestors of the Australian Aboriginals. Hundreds of years ago, Europeans began establishing settlements on what they used to call *Terra Australis Incognita* or "Unknown Southern Land."

However, for many years, Australia's history was believed to have begun in 1770. This was the year James Cook claimed the land for England, despite the fact that Australia had been discovered decades before by other European nations. On top of this, Australia was inhabited by the Aboriginals, who had been successfully living on the land for tens of thousands of years. The Aboriginals had developed complex political, spiritual, economic, and living rituals and systems. Each tribe was different, and their lifestyle mostly depended on the location. Contrary to stereotypes, not all groups were nomadic. By the time the Europeans had arrived, many Aboriginals had established permanent settlements, using agriculture for sustenance.

Europe's interest in Australia was reinvigorated due to the writings of a pirate, which intrigued geographers and administrators alike. In 1788, after decades of attempting to explore the Australian coast, which has some of the most dangerous waters in the world, the first

European settlement was formed. Australia, more specifically New South Wales, became a major British penal colony. Australia then transformed from one small penal colony to six colonies made up of mostly freed convicts and free people. The people gradually strayed from their British roots and formed their own culture.

After the Australian gold rush, the colonial government became responsible for the people's welfare. In 1901, Australia became a commonwealth, and it developed into a distinct nation with a rich culture. Eventually, mainly due to the world wars, Australia transformed into the nation it is today. However, until recently, its history was mostly unknown. After generations of misinformation, historians are working on uncovering the building blocks that led to the creation of modern-day Australia.

Chapter 1 – Prehistoric and Modern Aborigines of Australia (Around 60,000 Years Ago to the 16th Century)

Prehistoric Australia

Australia's history began long before England's Captain James Cook discovered Australia for Great Britain. It began long before the continent's first Aboriginals set foot on the land.

Modern-day Australia is known for having large, unique animals. However, around 250 to 65 million years ago, before any of those creatures reached the continent, there was actually a diverse range of prehistoric animals and dinosaurs that roamed the land. In 2007, a skeleton was discovered that stumped paleontologists for years. It was not until over a decade later that it was identified as a 2-story tall (16.4 to 21.3 feet), basketball-court long (82 to 98.4 feet) dinosaur, possibly a *Brachiosaurus.*

Until this discovery, Australia's prehistoric history was mostly unknown. However, with the strides in paleontology made in the past few years, it is expected that much more of Australia's early history will be uncovered in the coming years.

The Nauwalabila I and Madjedbebe Archaeological Sites

Many millions of years later, long after dinosaurs went extinct, Australia's first inhabitants arrived from Southeast Asia. The actual date of their arrival is heavily debated by historians, as some believe that the first people of Australia arrived around thirty thousand years ago, while others contest that Australia had human inhabitants around eighty thousand years ago.

The Nauwalabila I archaeological site, located in the Northern Territory of Australia, is a rock shelter. It appeared to be covered in charcoal and ash. Scientists attempted to date the site using radiocarbon dating. However, the carbon-14 dating technique proved to be inconclusive. This means the site is over fifty thousand years old. Subsequent studies were performed, including the optically stimulated luminescence (OSL) technique. As the name implies, it tests the last time the site, specifically the sand, was exposed to sunlight. These results revealed that the site might be at least fifty-three thousand to sixty thousand years old. While the OSL test cannot give exact dates of when humans inhabited the rock shelter, there is no doubt that Nauwalabila I had human activity, which would have moved the sand in and around the site.

More can be discovered about the continent's original people from Nauwalabila I than just their time of arrival. The rock shelter had layers of ash and charcoal, which indicate that campfires were made near it. Furthermore, animal bones, shells, stone tools, and spear points were discovered throughout the site. On the walls of Nauwalabila I, there are faded paintings that were likely made with ochre, which is a clay rock that was commonly used for cave paintings throughout Australia. Sandstone was discovered around the shelter with wear from grinding. This has led historians and scientists to conclude that the first people ground ochre clay on sandstone until it became a powder that could be used as paint. It is likely that this paint was not only used for painting walls but also for painting human bodies for ceremonial purposes.

The Madjedbebe archaeological site, also located in the Northern Territory of Australia, displays similar findings as Nauwalabila I. Evidence of ochre grinding, paintings, food remains, tools (namely stone axes), stone spear tips, mortars, pestles, and other grinding tools were found at the site. After performing a similar series of tests, the Madjedbebe site was dated at around the same time as Nauwalabila I. However, close to thirty years after these dates were uncovered, further OSL tests led experts to believe that the Madjedbebe rock shelter may have been inhabited as early as sixty-five thousand to eighty thousand years ago.

If the findings of the Nauwalabila I and Madjedbebe archaeological sites are accurate, that would mean that Australia's first humans arrived during the Pleistocene Epoch. This was the most recent ice age, and it lasted for over two million years, ending almost twelve thousand years ago. During the Pleistocene Epoch, much of the planet was still covered in ice, meaning that the water levels were lower since the ice had not yet melted into the oceans. Assuming this was the case, the Sahul Shelf, which refers to the area between the northern coast of Australia and the southern coast of Papua New Guinea, may have actually been land that is now flooded. This is similar to the Bering Strait land bridge, which was believed to have connected Russia to Alaska.

Before the end of the ice age, the Sahul Shelf is believed by some to have been entirely traversable, allowing humans to walk to Australia from Asia. The first people of Australia were believed to have actually come from what is now Malaysia, Singapore, Brunei, East Timor, Indonesia, and the Philippines. Reaching Australia from these territories by foot would also mean that the Sunda Shelf would have existed. In theory, it was identical to the Sahul Shelf, as it was a landmass that is now flooded due to raised sea levels. However, it would have been enveloped much of Southeast Asia.

Assuming the OSL tests dating the Madjedbebe archaeological site are accurate, this would mean that modern *Homo sapiens* reached Australia before Europe. Of course, the findings at both Nauwalabila I and Madjedbebe are contested, as termites have been known to disturb rock shelters by tunneling. They push tools, sand, and rock fragments deeper down into the earth, making them seem older. Furthermore, some historians and scientists are even skeptical about the early people of Australia's arrival by land. While there very likely was a land bridge or land that is now flooded, historians debate exactly how much of this area was water and how much was traversable land. According to various historians and scientists, some form of watercraft must have been used for part of the trip, specifically between Bali and Lombok and between Timor and Greater Australia. While there may have been other waterways throughout the Sahul and Sunda Shelves, these two stretches are over 200 kilometers (124 miles) in distance, meaning unless there were little islands scattered about, swimming was not an option. This would mean that Australia's first people were the first to travel nautically known to date, as it would date human seafaring and watercraft construction as early as sixty thousand years ago.

The Aborigines of Australia

Regardless of how exactly the first people, known as Aborigines, arrived, it is certain that they reached Australia before the end of the ice age. This means the sea levels were lower and that there was some land exposed that is flooded today. Since the Pleistocene Epoch is estimated to have ended 11,700 years ago, that would mean that the Aborigines of Australia have inhabited the continent for at least that long.

Historians can almost entirely confirm that the Aborigines have been in Australia for at least thirty thousand years. However, it is heavily contested if they occupied the continent much earlier than that, as you will discover for yourself. Keep in mind that the years mentioned in this chapter are still very much in flux, so nothing is truly known for certain. We have compiled the most accurate guesses as of now, but these will more than likely change as more testing is done.

It is estimated that around twenty thousand years ago (some historians argue this happened earlier, between thirty-five thousand years ago), the Aborigines spread throughout mainland Australia, specifically around the coasts and Tasmania. They were able to reach Tasmania easily at this time since it was not yet an island. It would not become one until around 13,500 to 8,000 years ago, when the water levels rose.

Until around eighteen thousand years ago, the interior of Australia, which still has some of the most extreme climates in the world, was essentially uninhabitable. While the Aborigines likely settled temporarily in these regions, it would not be until around ten thousand years ago that the first permanent settlements were made there.

While little is known about the Aborigines before the Common Era began around this time. Through archaeological discoveries, historians and scientists have been able to learn about the activities of the first people of Australia. At the Madjedbebe archaeological site, there was evidence of proper human burials that date back tens of thousands of years. Other archaeological findings have been uncovered. For instance, it has been learned that many bodies were purposefully cremated as early as forty thousand years ago. These two findings indicate that the Aborigines of Australia not only had post-death rituals but likely also some form of spiritual beliefs. The latter theory is also reinforced by the fact that there has been evidence of personal ornamentation, as it seems the people used shells as beads and painted their bodies with ochre pigment.

Experts have been able to confirm that trade existed amongst the first tribes, though it probably did not come into play until around ten thousand years ago. The Aboriginal people seemed to live in a variety of living structures, not just rock shelters like Madjedbebe and

Nauwalabila I. Since many tribes were nomadic, the Aboriginals often slept next to wind-blocking structures with a simple campfire. Temporary wood structures were made by laying branches, twisting canes, and covering them with leaves. These were quite common as well. Evidence shows that a tribe's living structures, lifestyle, and diet really depended on its climate and landscape. Unfortunately, until the climate of the interior settled and the Aborigines spread throughout the continent, most of the settlements were made along the coast. These were flooded after the end of the ice age, destroying evidence of how the first people lived.

Diets of the First People of Australia

Luckily, some evidence survived the floods, such as fishing traps, animal bones, stone tools, and stone shelters, that were displaced but not destroyed. Shell middens, which are essentially trash heaps composed mostly of the debris of shellfish after humans had consumed the meat, have proven to be some of the most important discoveries for advancing historians' understanding of prehistoric humans. In addition to shellfish, the remains of other animal bones were often thrown in the heap.

The remains in the heap can be used to date the settlement through radiocarbon testing. The shell middens of many locations revealed that most Aboriginal tribes, even those dating back thousands of years, were hunter-gatherer fishing societies. It seems they relied heavily on aquatic animals for their diet. Those along the coast mainly ate seafood, which included large dolphins, sharks, turtles, rays, and a variety of fish. Whales were also apparently eaten, although it is unlikely that they were caught. They were most likely eaten and used for various purposes when they washed up on shore. In northern Australia, in addition to some of the aforementioned aquatic life, Aboriginal people hunted sea cows, known as dugong, and saltwater crocodiles. Those scattered in Australia's interior, away from the coasts, still had diets that relied heavily on aquatic animals. Inland tribes would hunt and eat freshwater fish, turtles, crayfish, prawns, crocodiles, and eels.

The style of fishing and hunting really depended on the prey and location. On the coast, spearing and scoop nets were used in shallow waters. In deep waters, they used canoes and harpoons, cane fish traps with meat as bait, and fishing lines, which were made with string lines with sharp shells as a hook. In northern Australia, evidence of stone fish traps has been found, which required the understanding of the tides to catch fish well. Similar methods were used inland in rivers but without the canoes, which were not commonly used in the shallow streams.

Besides seafood, Australia's first people were known to consume a variety of birds, insects, reptiles, amphibians, fruits, nuts, seeds, vegetables, and mushrooms. As mentioned above, their diet depended greatly on what was available in their surroundings. After years of survival, the Aboriginals developed an incredible understanding of the flora and fauna in their environments, and tribes could survive in even the harshest climates. Food was not prepared as they are today, especially in the areas where it was harder to come by. Toxic nuts, known as cycad fruits, were soaked until their poisons were removed. Seeds were collected, ground, and cooked on coals to create bush breads. While some of these recipes have been continued by today's Aboriginal descendants, most of their food preparation and collection techniques are no longer practical.

Aboriginal Lifestyles, Systems, and Beliefs

As the Aborigines spread throughout Australia, they began to separate into smaller groups and develop distinctive social systems, beliefs, and structures that were unique from other Aboriginal tribes. The differences between the tribes' lifestyles really depended on the following factors: their geographical location, their population, their religious/totemic beliefs, and their social structure.

Geographical Location and Population

Generally, an Australian Aboriginal population could be broken down into tribes, which are a group of people who speak the same language and live in the same location. A tribe can be broken down further into a band or a horde, which is usually made up of a few families that form an alliance for survival. They might aid each other in gathering food, protecting each other, or helping raise each other's children. Over the course of thousands of years, nomadic bands of twenty or so members who spoke the same language would group together and form increasingly larger tribes. By the time the Europeans arrived in Australia, Aboriginal tribes usually had a population of around 450 people, but they could have as many as 600 people or more.

While some tribes co-inhabited land with other tribes or shared land, tribes generally had some form of border around their claimed land. This border was usually natural, such as mountains or rivers. Since a tribe's territory was generally quite large, the bands could usually find enough food within their tribe's territory. That being said, if tribes were friendly with their neighboring tribes, it was not uncommon for populations to travel into each other's land.

While tribes were formed based on language, the Australian Aboriginals, even thousands of years ago, were multilingual unless they were completely isolated from other tribes, which was uncommon. Tribes often shared words with their neighboring tribes' languages. The farther people traveled from their homes, the more difficult it would be to converse. For the most part, tribes would either be fluent in the languages of their neighboring tribes or have enough words in common to communicate. Over the years, this led to trade relationships and alliances.

Of course, relationships were not always so positive. Boundaries were fought over, especially when food was harder to come by. Wars were just as common thousands of years ago as they were when the Europeans arrived in Australia. The biggest difference was weapons.

The Aboriginals were not as advanced in this arena, which meant their weapons were not as deadly.

Languages and diets were not the only things that differed due to their geographical location. Tribes that lived close to each other often had lots in common. The farther one traveled, the more extreme the differences would be, kind of like countries or state lines today. Two tribes that lived far enough apart could be so different that they might speak different languages, look different, and believe in different religions. On top of this, they might even have different baskets, beds, and structures. In other words, two tribes that lived far away from each other could very well have absolutely nothing in common.

Baskets are a perfect example, as Aboriginal tribes created different baskets depending on their location. In northern Australia and along the coast, where it rains often, trees grow with stringy and fibrous bark and roots that can be easily spun into string. This string was then used to create open mesh-style baskets, which resembled bags. In Australia's interior, which is mostly desert, string was made from human hair, animal fur, and grass stalks. For weapons, stronger strings were made from kangaroo tendons. In some cases, it was just more practical to create wooden baskets or bowls for gathering food.

Religion and Totemic Structuring

Geographical location influenced almost every aspect of Australian Aboriginal life, as did religion, which was also influenced by location. It was common for religious deities to be inspired by local conditions. For example, those living in northern Australia and along the coast, where torrential rain is common, often had deities connected to the skies, thunder, lightning, and rain. In the desert, in Australia's interior, where weather was mostly arid, deities were often modeled more after animals or humans.

Australia's Aboriginal religious leaders, known as totems, totemic beings, or ancestral beings, were usually emblematic. Thus, it was very common for a tribe's geography to be represented in their religious beliefs. People would consider their totem to be their ancestor, so it was common for tribes to be divided into groups depending on their specific ancestral being. For example, in northern Kimberley, the Aboriginal population divided themselves into two groups, which are known as *moieties*: the Wodoi (the spotted nightjar) and Djungun (the owlet nightjar).

This was based on a story where two bird-men fought during Dreamtime. Dreamtime refers to a period of time tens of thousands of years ago. This is when Aboriginal people believed their ancestors first came to the continent and shaped it into what it became. According to the Artlandish Aboriginal Art Gallery located in Western Australia, it is referred to as the Dreamtime because "It conveys better the timeless concept of moving from 'dream' to reality which in itself is an act of creation and the basis of many Aboriginal creation myths." Dreamtime embodies the past, present, and future, as it encapsulates all facets of life. It encompasses the time, people, and the land, as well as what happens during one's life and after a person's physical death.

In some tribes, the population was divided into even more than two groups. The populations were sometimes divided into groups of four, which are known as sections. Those were further divided into groups of eight or more, known as subsections. Aboriginals would refer to their group that they were born into as their skin name, which was usually named after religious totems. They were often names of plants or animals, although totems could also be named after inanimate objects as well. A person could not switch their group or skin name, and they could not even marry someone from a different group. Much like religions today, people of different totems could be found in different tribes and locations. Those with the same skin name would instantly find kinship, even if they barely spoke the same language. In this way, totemic beliefs aided in forming alliances between tribes and structuring society by deciding who one could marry.

Another way religion helped to structure tribes was in terms of land ownership and boundaries. According to most Aboriginal beliefs, people do not own land. Rather, they belong to the land, which is controlled by the totems. In tribes where this belief is still upheld, boundary lines are often undefined since land should not be owned by any specific tribe. However, in other tribes, the belief that the land belongs to the totems of ancestral beings is upheld since the population has a responsibility to uphold the land, known as a clan estate. They have to visit the sacred sites, keep them clean, repaint paintings, and perform spiritual rituals. The person responsible for maintaining the integrity of the ancestral lands is known as the clan leader, who is often a senior. Since ancestral beings live in trees, mountains, rocks, or other elements in nature, these sacred locations are often an important factor in the division of clan estates. Since clan estates were often divided with spiritual intention and since the people did not identify by territory but by their totem, war was usually uncommon.

As previously mentioned, the Dreamtime refers to the past, present, and future. Aboriginals believed that there was a sort of blueprint to life, which included ceremonies that connected themselves to their ancestral beings. While there were rituals throughout one's whole life that were thought to affect virtually every aspect of life, one of the most important Aboriginal ceremonies was that of children becoming adults. Week-long celebrations of storytelling, ceremonial dancing, singing, and decorating were important to connect children to their ancestral beings as they transitioned into adulthood. Dreams were also an important aspect of Aboriginal religion, as they were seen as ways for spirits to connect with living people and transfer messages to aid with survival from their ancestral beings.

Much like today, religious beliefs helped the Aboriginal people survive, even when life was at its hardest. Their belief in ancestral beings, deities, and ritualistic blueprints helped them to gain control of their surroundings and fight to continue living even in the most extreme conditions.

Funeral ceremonies and burial practices date back tens of thousands of years. These rituals vary greatly from tribe to tribe; however, it was common for funeral attendees to wear some form of ceremonial clothing or body paint. They would sing, dance, tell stories, and even cut themselves in order to feel for their lost loved ones and to aid in the passing of their spirit. In some parts of Australia, there were two burials, which ensured the spirit of the person who had passed left its burial location and made it back to its original place of birth. The first burial involved leaving the body on a piece of wood for months under natural cover, such as leaves. By the time of the second burial, only the bones would remain. They were collected, often painted, and then dispersed. Every tribe and skin name had different ways to disperse bones. Other religious rituals were physical; for example, circumcision was quite common throughout Australian Aboriginal tribes. The tribes' rituals varied and included piercings, teeth pulling, cutting, hair removal, fire markings, and hymen cutting.

Family and Political Organization

In most Aboriginal beliefs, children were born through their parents, and a spirit from the Dreamtime would bring the fetus to life. Kinship was important right from birth, as the child was raised not only around their parents but also members of their entire family, band, and tribe. The sister of one's mother was generally also known as mother, not as an aunt. The same applied to their uncles. The same relationship was common for nephews or nieces; all children in the same generation were raised together as if they were siblings.

Just like religion, kinship had a strict blueprint that detailed how certain members of the family should act around one another, even down to the types of humor they could share and whether or not they could argue. For example, brothers and sisters were not very close, and men and their mothers-in-law (as well as his aunts-in-law, who were also known as mothers-in-law) had to avoid each other. These rules may seem extreme. However, they kept families bonded together because fighting or being inappropriate not only went against one's relationship with relatives but also one's religious beliefs. These rules generally did not apply to children until they were transitioning into adulthood. Generally, they would be a teenager, though the age one transitioned to an adult varied greatly from location to location.

Arranged marriages, even for infants, were common, as was reciprocity, in which case two families were linked by marriages to the extent that some family members might even be exchanged. The actual terms of marriage differed greatly in each tribe and ancestral family. Some tribes only counted a marriage as valid until a child was born; once that happened, they could find a new partner and have more children with them. In some areas of Australia, polygyny was practiced. However, both of these practices were generally more because of practical purposes than religious ones. In terms of the latter, polygyny was often beneficial since it could increase the amount of food a certain family could bring in. From a young age, children would also accompany their parents on food-gathering trips in order to learn and bring in more food for the family.

Similar to the breakdown of kinship, where all men a generation older were known as fathers, tribes did not have a "chief." Although there was a political structure, most Aboriginal societies were classless and egalitarian. That being said, gender and age usually played a part in one's rights and power. Without a political leader, socialization was necessary, which refers to self-regulation in society for fear of shame and punishment. Since the tribes were mostly nomadic, crimes were minimal since time was mostly spent hunting and gathering food.

Aboriginal Lifestyle

Although every tribe and band had its own patterns, systems, and lifestyles, in general, Australian Aboriginals followed one of the following two lifestyles. First, in the fertile regions around coastal or exterior Australia, camps were established near sacred locations and practical resources, such as running water. Most of the day was spent away from camp, searching for food. In some cases, hunters would spend multiple days chasing prey, but generally, the people returned home at night. Although camps were inhabited for months at a time, the bands were not sedentary since home bases were moved for sacred rituals, a lack of food, threats, changing weather, or other reasons.

The second lifestyle was found in less fertile territories, mostly in the deserts in Australia's interior. Bands in arid regions were much more nomadic than those in fertile ones, as they rarely stayed in one location for longer than a few days unless the season was perfect and the watering hole large enough to support the population. Since water was hard to come by in Australia's interior, bands traveled in small groups and only slept by a watering hole for a few days before moving on.

All Aboriginal people had few material objects, and any item that wasn't practical was religious. Tribes mostly carried around tools, such as multi-purpose tools for digging, hunting, or carrying things. Larger tools, such as stones used for cooking food or grinding paint pigment, were usually left behind.

Obligations mostly depended on one's age and gender. The women cared for the children and gathered food; they were estimated to have gathered at least 60 percent of all the food. Men hunted for meat, which was necessary to provide protein for the tribe. When they became too old, they usually stopped working these physically taxing tasks and transitioned into caring for the sacred land and leading rituals. Since bands were nomadic, they often encountered other bands, either within their own tribe or neighboring tribes. When two tribes or bands met, it was common to exchange gifts and trade various practical items and foods. That being said, Australia's Aboriginals never established any formal markets or trading hubs. Trading was done casually between a few people. Even though trading was not widespread, items from one side of Australia eventually reached the other side of the continent since nomadic tribes traded items amongst themselves. It is said that items essentially crisscrossed Australia, and they usually went in the direction of the tribes' movements.

Prehistoric Versus Modern Aboriginal Australians

While historians have been able to uncover a lot of evidence confirming the activities of prehistoric Aboriginal populations, much of what we know about Australia's first people has been based on modern-day Aboriginal populations and orally transmitted stories. All of this is complicated by the fact that experts are still unsure whether Australia's Aborigines arrived in multiple waves or not. Although it is known that everyone who ever stepped foot in Australia was a *Homo sapien*, there still would be extreme physical differences between a first-wave person, who arrived likely over forty thousand years ago, and people who arrived only fifteen thousand years ago.

This theory that there were multiple waves of immigrants is supported by the skulls found throughout the continent. Some experts believe that the differences in skulls may actually be due to body rituals that involve deforming one's head, although others believe it shows there were two different waves. Either way, these differences prove how different one tribe was from another. It is estimated there may have been around 500 distinctive tribes and over 300,000 Aboriginals throughout Australia at the beginning of European occupation.

Much of their lifestyles and structures that have been mentioned previously in this book are known to still exist amongst Australian Aboriginals today. They have been proven to have existed for hundreds, if not thousands, of years. However, the exact year of when they began is uncertain. While evidence of human burials, body painting, and tool crafting have been dated to over fifty thousand years ago, it is unknown exactly how these practices evolved over the years and how the Aboriginals began to separate, spread out over Australia, and build their distinctive cultures.

Whether or not more waves of people immigrated into Australia is unknown; however, what is known for sure is that various waves of animals immigrated to the continent over the years. For example, the dingo, which is an Australian wild dog originally from Southeast Asia, is said to have only arrived in Australia around five thousand to three thousand years ago. Since the land bridges were already flooded by this point, it is likely that dingoes were introduced into Australia by Asian sailors.

When the Aborigines first arrived in Australia, the continent looked completely different than today. Not only was the climate and coastline different due to the ice age, but the topography, flora, and fauna were completely different as well. It is believed that prehistoric humans existed with megafaunas, such as the giant wombat and the giant *Megalania* (a massive reptile). Whether or not the human occupation of Australia is directly responsible for the extinction of these megafaunas and the change in territories is unknown. Some experts believe that after around twenty thousand years of human habitation, Australia looked completely different. For example, Australia's interior may not have once been so barren and arid, and it is thought that many species of animals were completely wiped out. That being said, other historians believe this was due to climate change.

Regardless of why the landscape and nature changed in Australia, this surely would have impacted the way of life of the Aborigines. One example of how the Aboriginal people changed by the time of European occupation was the presence of sedentary tribes. There is still little evidence of this existing in their earlier history. By the 18th century, sedentary Aboriginal groups had developed advanced agriculture, as well as irrigation techniques and fisheries. While there were, of course, still nomadic tribes who lived more similarly to the prehistoric tribes, it is possible that the extinction of animals and the change in the landscape forced the tribes to settle down and develop agricultural techniques in order to survive.

Chapter 2 – First Contact and European Explorations (16th Century to 19th Century)

Although Willem Janszoon was the first European explorer to set foot in Australia, the continent had been discovered by Europeans long before. It was likely even visited by other explorers. Chinese and Arab texts both vaguely detail a landmass to the south, which has led historians to theorize that Australia was discovered and perhaps even visited as early as the 1400s. Of course, Asian seafarers would have visited Australia long before, as is obvious with the appearance of dingoes. However, the first actual documentation of Australia in the modern age is not until the 16th century. Since there were Asian settlements not even five hundred kilometers away from Australia, it would not be surprising that they were aware of the land. By the 18th century, Indonesian Makassarese were known to fish in the Northern Territory of Australia; however, it is not certain when exactly this practice began.

European Exploration

By the 16th century, the race for European exploration had begun. The primary motives for European conquest at this time can be separated into three categories: God, gold, and glory. God, or the spreading of religious beliefs, proved to be an important motive for European exploration. Most expeditions included tens, if not hundreds, of missionaries who intended to convert any people they encountered. Gold not only refers to the possibility of finding gold and other profitable resources to exploit but also the potential to discover water passages that would facilitate trade. Kings and companies were known to fund expeditions throughout the Atlantic and Pacific in order to find new trade routes. Finally, European nations were motivated by competition with one another—glory. Even as early as the 14th century, Spain and Portugal were competing to colonize and explore as much of the world as quickly as possible, which explains why they were the first two European nations to come close to making contact with Australia.

Although there is no actual evidence proving the Portuguese set foot in Australia, it is believed that slaves were gathered from Australia's Melville Island. Some historians do believe that the Portuguese may have been the first Europeans to discover Australia. The Portuguese and other European nations referred to the landmass as *Terra Australis Incognita*, which means "Unknown Southern Land." This name is said to have actually been given to the landmass as early as the 5th century by the Romans. Of course, at this time, the Europeans had no idea of the lands this far south. To them, it made sense that if there were lands in the north, there had to be more lands in the south. *Australis* was present on maps as early as the 1520s.

As can be inferred, *Australis* is actually the namesake for Australia's current name, which was simply an adjustment to "southern" made by Matthew Flinders, an 18th-century British explorer. By the 16th century, European nations had already begun to explore parts of the Americas, and the first permanent Spanish settlement had been founded in 1493. In 1567, it is believed that the Solomon Islands were discovered by a Spanish expedition led by Álvaro de Mendaña, which left from Peru. According to texts from the time, Álvaro de Mendaña attempted to relocate the Solomon Islands in 1595; however, he was unsuccessful. While it is uncertain whether or not Álvaro de Mendaña actually disembarked in Oceania or not, he certainly opened up European consciousness to the region.

Pedro Fernández de Quirós, who was a Portuguese-born, Spanish-employed officer of Mendaña, felt it was important to attempt to relocate the southern land. So, he commanded an expedition leaving from Peru in 1605 in search of *Terra Australis Incognita*. In December of that year, he was successful in reaching New Hebrides, a group of islands located east of Queensland, which at the time was inhabited by Aboriginal populations. He named his discovery *Australia del Espíritu Santo*, or "Southland of the Holy Spirit." However, he did not have time to colonize the islands since he had to return to the Americas. Afterward, Spanish explorers were unable to earn the backing to fund another expedition to *Terra Australis Incognita*.

Dutch Exploration of Terra Australis Incognita

The same year as Fernández de Quirós's expedition to *Terra Australis Incognita*, the Dutch sent an expedition led by Willem Janszoon in search of New Guinea. After leaving Batam, which was at this time part of the Dutch East Indies, Janszoon was instructed to explore New Guinea for economic opportunities. This region had long been in the consciousness of European nations since it had been discovered by Portuguese explorers decades before. After reaching the southern coast of New Guinea, he continued sailing south, expecting to follow the New Guinea coastline. Instead, he arrived in what he named Cape Keerweer, which would have been located in the north of Queensland in Australia. Although the documentation is vague, it is believed that Janszoon and his men disembarked at Cape Keerweer, where they got into violent altercations with the Aboriginal population there and were forced to sail back north. If this is accurate, it would mean that this was the first example of contact between the Europeans and the indigenous population of Australia.

When Dutch ships began traveling to and from Java (now a part of Indonesia), it was common for captains to miss the small islands by a bit since navigation and cartography were not entirely accurate. When the ships ended up slightly east, they reached Australia, an error that occurred many times starting in 1616 with explorer Dirk Hartog. Hartog ended up in Western Australia, becoming the first European to explore that region of the continent. For a time, a portion of Australia was named *Eendrachtland* after Dirk Hartog's ship, the *Eendracht*. Hartog would not be the only Dutch captain to reach Australia. Over the course of the next decade or so, various seafarers would disembark and explore the coastline of Australia.

Ten years after Hartog reached Western Australia, explorer Pieter Nuyts traveled over 1,600 kilometers (994 miles) along the southern coastline of Australia. With his work and that of other explorers who traversed the northern and western coasts, the Europeans significantly improved their understanding of the landmass that was once unknown.

Although notable work was accomplished by his predecessors, it would be Abel Tasman, who joined the Dutch East India Company in the early 1630s, who would contribute the most significant information for the Europeans' understanding of Australia. After serving the Dutch East India Company on expeditions to Japan, Cambodia, Taiwan, and Sumatra, the company chose Tasman to be the commander of the next expedition, which would be the most ambitious journey for the Dutch at that time. Abel Tasman was assigned the hefty task of mapping Australia, as at this point, it was still unknown whether the landmass was connected to other continents. All known expeditions that had reached Australia had embarked from the east and traveled west. Tasman was instructed to travel west to east with the hopes that he would uncover new lands and shorter travel routes to South America.

In late November of 1642, Tasman, who was traveling east from Mauritius, first discovered Tasmania, which explains the name.

However, at the time, he named it Van Diemen's Land after the governor-general of the Dutch East Indies. In early December, he decided to act on his original instructions and did not explore modern-day Tasmania any further. Instead, he continued eastward with his expedition, which led Tasman and his ships to New Zealand. After exploring the coastlines for a few weeks, he set sail again on January 4th. He believed New Zealand was somehow connected to South America. Before completing his expedition, Tasman discovered Tonga and the Fiji Islands. He managed to explore much of Oceania without ever reaching Australia itself.

Although Abel Tasman was quite successful in discovering lands, the Dutch East India Company felt he had not completed his assigned task of exploring the main southern landmass or discovering whether a water passage to South America, specifically Chile, existed. In 1644, Tasman was sent on another journey, specifically to explore New Guinea, Van Diemen's Land (Tasmania), Western Australia, and the rest of Australia. Leaving in late February from Batavia (Indonesia), Tasman followed the southern coast of New Guinea and began sailing into the Torres Strait, thinking it was a bay. Once he reached the main landmass, Tasman followed the Australian coast along the Gulf of Carpentaria, making his way along the northern and then western coasts. Before returning home, Tasman named Australia's main landmass as New Holland.

While Tasman once again contributed great strides to the Dutch understanding of Australia, or New Holland, the Dutch East India Company was once again disappointed upon his return. While the landmass had been significantly mapped out, the Dutch East India Company was mainly focused on the profits that could be gained from new lands. Tasman's journey had failed to reveal any new economic opportunities. According to Tasman, as well as other previous and subsequent explorers who reached New Holland, the region did not seem ideal for colonization, as the settlements depended on agriculture. The soil did not seem fertile, there was a lack of water, and, on top of that, the indigenous population was aggressive and uninviting.

British Interest in Terra Australis and New Holland

Over the next few decades, the Netherlands would lose interest in *Terra Australis Incognita*. However, after the significant discoveries were made by Dutch explorers, other Europeans were made aware of the landmass. In the 1660s, a French geographer created a map that featured New Holland, as well as *Terra Australis*. In 1688, an English pirate named William Dampier visited Australia. He is believed to have traveled a few hundred kilometers around the coast. Over the subsequent years, William Dampier published *A New Voyage Round the World*, which touched on his time in New Holland. He attempted to convince the English government and companies to send explorers to New Holland and *Terra Australis*. Despite his beliefs that Australia was worth revisiting, his negative description of the land and local population, which was in line with that of the previous Dutch explorers, did not work well in convincing England to send expensive and dangerous expeditions to explore the land.

Over the subsequent years, various European explorers, companies, writers, and geographers would continue to be interested in *Terra Australis Incognita*. Finally, after many decades, the British government decided to fund multiple expeditions to discover whether there was any potential for economic opportunities and settlements in New Holland and *Terra Australis*.

British Voyages and James Cook

James Cook, who was born in 1728 in Yorkshire, England, became the apprentice of a shipowner at eighteen, where he learned all of the skills necessary to travel the open seas, including basic sailing and mathematics. Cook would become a mate and join the British Royal Navy, where he displayed incredible seamanship skills and impressed his superiors. Cook would continue to advance in rank until the Seven Years' War. He became the captain of a seized ship, and he was able to further prove his abilities.

In the subsequent years after the end of the war, James Cook would continue to command and sail ships. Some of the details of his trips, including the observation of an eclipse, were sent to the Royal Society in London, which led it to choose Cook as a commander for an expedition to the South Pacific in 1768. Cook was given the HMS *Endeavour* and instructed to lead some members of the Royal Society to Tahiti. They would then continue on to explore *Terra Australis*. Since this was over a century after Abel Tasman's discoveries, philosophers, geographers, and explorers were not even sure that landmasses even existed.

Cook and his crew, which included lead scientist Joseph Banks and his assistant Daniel Solander, left England in August of 1768 and finally left Tahiti in June of the following year. First, Cook located New Zealand. After six months of sailing the coasts and exploring the land, he completed a map of New Zealand. Cook continued on sailing and searching for the southern landmass. Finally, on April 19th, 1770, he reached Australia's southeastern coast. The voyage continued traveling north along Australia's eastern coast. This over 3,000-kilometer trek included traversing the Great Barrier Reef in Queensland through the Coral Sea, which is still considered to be one of the most challenging areas in the world to sail. In fact, the obstacles in that area are so hazardous that the ship came close to sinking when it came into contact with some coral. However, Cook managed to get it to shore and repair it.

Although most of James Cook's journey took place on the sea, his ship did have to land, which he did at both Botany Bay and Possession Island. Those stops led to the naming of New South Wales. After continuing on through the Torres Strait, Cook and all those on the HMS *Endeavour* made a brief stop in Batavia (Jakarta) and then continued home to England.

On top of accomplishing the missions set out by the Royal Society and rediscovering Australia, Cook is renowned for his protocols as a captain. He was known to enforce specific diets that actually resulted in no deaths of scurvy, which was common for seafarers at the time. This voyage was also important since it was one of the first expeditions that put an emphasis on science and sent scientific leaders abroad. In 1772, James Cook began his second expedition, this time even more south to Antarctica. His discoveries of New Caledonia, the South Sandwich Islands, and South Georgia Island, as well as his charting of Tonga and Easter Island, proved that Australia was not connected to any other landmass. After returning home, Cook embarked on one final mission in 1776 to explore the waters between Canada and Russia by way of the Pacific. This journey would be his last, as he was killed after an altercation in Hawaii.

Subsequent Explorations

In 1786, plans to create a settlement in New Holland began. Two years later, the settlement was formed. However, despite forming a settlement and the fact that James Cook made great strides in exploring Australia and Oceania, much of the landmass ultimately remained unknown. This was because all of the explorations had been done from the waters. Few men had actually spent longer than a day or two on land.

As Australia's first settlement was forming, explorers continued to visit Australia and worked on mapping out what was still unknown. After the work done by Cook, *Terra Australis Incognita* was not only of interest to Britain but other European nations as well. In the following years, French explorer Marion du Fresne explored Tasmania, and the Count of La Pérouse visited Botany Bay. Britain's George Vancouver continued exploring the southern coastline, and Joseph-Antoine Raymond de Bruni visited Tasmania. Over the following years, more explorations were made that helped to map out what was a once unknown land, the most notable of which occurred after the end of the 18th century.

At this point, the name of Australia was still New Holland, despite not having been seriously revisited by the Netherlands since the mid-17th century. However, the lack of European interest in the region was about to change. British George Bass and Matthew Flinders, a naval surgeon and an officer, respectively, explored more of New Holland in 1795 and 1796. Over the following years, the two would make great strides in charting the landmass and would actually be the ones to officially declare that Tasmania was an island. In 1801, Flinders was assigned to completely chart the perimeter of New Holland to determine whether it was officially an island or not. Flinders's expedition lasted three years, and he determined that New Holland was officially an island. Therefore, since there was no more southern land, he requested that the name be formally changed to Australia, which was backed by the government in 1817. The landmass was still referred to as New Holland for many years, and it would not be until many decades later that it began to lose its association with its old name.

Although Flinders had completely mapped out the perimeter of Australia, some of the coastlines were a little unclear, as he did not hug the coast for safety reasons. Over the subsequent years, explorers would continue to work on charting the landmass, with the most notable work after Flinders being done by Phillip Parker King and John Clements Wickham, who helped to map out the coastline between Arnhem Land and the Cape York Peninsula. Other nations, mainly France, would continue to attempt to explore what was once known as *Terra Australis Incognita*. However, after the creation of Great Britain's first settlement in New Holland in 1788, the landmass was officially claimed by Britain.

Chapter 3 – European Colonization and Settling in Australia (1788)

Of course, as established in Chapter 1, the land was inhabited by the Aboriginal population long before Britain claimed Australia as its own. But even though Europe had known about Australia prior to England's claim, little was done to form settlements because it was deemed infertile, unlivable, and unprofitable by various nations. However, the Aboriginal people of Australia had not only found ways to survive in the harsh climates but also to form settlements of their own, which included developing agriculture to suit the region. One example of an agricultural practice used by Aboriginal people was burning massive areas of land to help clear out forests, making hunting easier. It also promoted the growth of plants, which benefited from the additional space, light, and nutrients from the ashes in the soil.

New South Wales Settlement

In 1770, New South Wales was claimed by James Cook for the British, making it the first European colony in New Holland. The first formal discussions of creating a settlement in New South Wales began in 1786, although the British government had been considering populating the region for a while by that point. Despite seeming unprofitable and being difficult to reach, colonizing Australia was of interest to Great Britain for multiple reasons. Firstly, Australia was out of easy reach from Europe; however, its proximity to Asia made it an interesting settlement since the British government planned to continue invading and acquiring Asian countries. For instance, India would be officially seized by Britain in 1858. Its proximity to Asia also facilitated trade with Asian countries, such as China. If Britain could create a trading post in Australia that could be easily accessed by Asian merchants, it would improve its trading position over other European countries.

Secondly, although New Holland had previously been deemed unprofitable, further exploration revealed the presence of lumber that could be used to build ships. The companies and the British government were willing to revisit the landmass; perhaps it had some economic potential that had not yet been discovered. Thirdly, it is believed that England wanted to construct a military fort in order to gain a powerful position when it came to war, which was commonplace in the 18th and 19th centuries, with Britain and other nations constantly invading and seizing territories. While all of the previously listed reasons served as motivators for creating a settlement in Australia, the main motivator for colonizing Australia was actually to use it as a penal colony.

Before creating the settlement in New South Wales, England had been using colonies in what would become the United States of America as penal colonies. Penal colonies, which served as a place to send prisoners outside of the country, were necessary, as Britain's prisons were quickly filling up. The sudden lack of space in Britain's prisons is said to be because unemployment was high in the 18th century. Stealing, a crime that would send one to prison, was often seen as necessary for survival. After years of rebellion, the United States of America declared its independence in 1776. Britain no longer had a place to send its exiled prisoners. Suddenly, it faced increased pressure to form a new settlement. Thus, the creation of the settlement in New South Wales was accelerated.

The settlement plans were organized by Thomas Townshend, who was known as Lord Sydney (hence the name of Australia's first settlement). Arthur Phillip, who had proved his seafaring skills by serving in the British navy, was assigned the task of commanding the expedition. He was instructed to claim the entire eastern coastline, from Cape York all the way to Tasmania, including the nearby islands. According to Lord Sydney, Arthur Phillip was to be the acting leader of the colony, and he was to "employ" the exiled prisoners to work on and develop the farms, thereby providing the British government with agricultural products and free labor. After being released from their sentence, former convicts would be allowed to own their own small amount of farming land, which they could use to feed themselves and earn a living.

On May 13th, 1787, Arthur Phillip led 11 ships, which included somewhere between 700 and 850 convicts and around 250 non-convicts, almost all of whom were marines prepared to act as jailers. On January 19th, 1788, the first ship arrived, and over the course of the next day, the rest of the vessels would arrive at Botany Bay, located on the southeastern coast of Australia. While the long voyage to Australia was overall successful, their good fortune stopped there, as Arthur Phillip ran into some unforeseen complications with Lord Sydney's plans.

As observed by previous explorers, Australia, specifically in the Botany Bay area where the first settlement was planned to be established, had infertile soil and a lack of water. The convicts and their jailers remained at Botany Bay while Phillip explored the coast for a better location to establish the colony. After a few days of sailing north, Phillip reached Port Jackson and decided to move the settlement to Sydney, which was an area that had not yet been traversed by European explorers. Phillip was reported to have sent a dispatch to Lord Sydney, advising his superior of his decision to move the settlement by saying, "We got into Port Jackson early in the afternoon, and had the satisfaction of finding the finest harbour in the world, in which a thousand sail of the line may ride in the most perfect security." The fleet was moved, and the British flag was raised on January 26th, 1788. This day is still celebrated as Australia Day, which is seen as controversial by many. After all, the continent was already inhabited by this point. Plus, the first European settlement was made up of convicts.

A few weeks later, a small group of people was sent to Norfolk Island in order to form another settlement. The colony on Norfolk Island would be abandoned by 1813; however, it was truly only created in order to keep the land under British control and to search for food.

Chapter 4 – The Beginning Years in the Settlements and the First Governors of the Colonies (1788 to 1810)

Governor Arthur Phillip (February 1788 to December 1792)

Over the next weeks, Phillip began fulfilling his role as governor and taking authority by following the directions given to him before leaving Lord Sydney. However, while Lord Sydney's plan may have been straightforward, accomplishing the task of establishing a successful settlement made up of only convicts and their jailers in a land none of the immigrants had visited previously was not easy.

The settlers knew very little about Australia itself, let alone how to survive in conditions that were so different from what they were used to. In the early years, the convicts struggled to farm the land. And since they barely harvested enough food for themselves, the British government was making little profit from their new settlement. On top of the food scarcity, diseases constantly broke out, which not only reduced the number of farmers able to take care of the plots but also threatened to eliminate the entire settlement. Smallpox, measles, and influenza were among some of the diseases that spread throughout the settlement and region within the first few years. However, it would not affect the British settlers as badly as it would the Australian Aboriginals, who had no antibodies against the European diseases. Considering that the new immigrants knew very little about the land at the time of their arrival, it is no surprise that they had so many unexpected issues, especially with the people who already inhabited the land.

Pests and dangerous animals posed constant threats since they were different from the creatures that existed in Europe. The humans caused even more conflicts. When Europe decided to form a settlement abroad, extensive planning went into where it was located, who would navigate the people there, who would govern the people once they arrived, and what people would be immigrating. However, it seems the government, companies, and settlers had vague plans on how to deal with the population that already existed there. This seemed to be the downfall of many previous European settlements, which either completely failed or came close to failing due to conflicts with the native populations. The same could be said about the Australian settlement.

Arthur Phillip did not seek to use hostilities when it came to the Australian Aboriginals, but of course, whether he was intentionally hostile or not, the governor was establishing a new population and government on land that the Aboriginal population did not have to previously share. Relations with the Aborigines were extremely negative, and although rebellions strained both sides, the Australian Aboriginals would suffer the most from the violence. According to a quote by Francis Tuckfield, who was a missionary, "A serious loss has been sustained by the natives without an equivalent being rendered. Their territory is not only invaded, but their game is driven back, their marnong and other valuable roots are eaten by the white man's sheep and their deprivation, abuse and miseries are daily increasing." Although Tuckfield was quoted saying this in 1837, the relationship between the Aboriginals and the settlers in the first years of colonization was no better.

On top of violence between the men for the land, settlers were violent toward the Aboriginal women and girls. Since few British women were sent to the new Australian settlement, settlers turned toward the Aboriginal females to satisfy their needs. This resulted in a massive increase in sexual abuse and exploitation. This ended up not only mentally traumatizing the Aboriginal population further but also physically traumatizing them, as venereal diseases were introduced into the native population. As mentioned previously, the British also spread their non-sexual diseases to the Aboriginal population, and smallpox, which was already deadly to the Europeans, turned out to be even more so for the Aborigines, who had no immunity. According to Arthur Phillip, it is estimated that nearly half the Aboriginal population in New South Wales died from catching smallpox alone. By the end of the 18th century, it is estimated that the native population of New South Wales had decreased by 90 percent since the arrival of British immigrants.

On top of having to deal with external conflicts and rebellions, Phillip had to manage internal issues, which were common with a population of convicts. That being said, the convicts were not necessarily the type who would be in modern jails. Historians often debate whether or not the population was really made up of "dangerous" criminals or simply those who broke the law to survive. Since most serious crimes, such as murder, would result in death, those who were imprisoned in Britain usually committed petty crimes, mostly theft and property crimes. Some were simply political prisoners who stood up against the authoritarian British government. Regardless of whether or not the group were truly criminals or just misunderstood and mistreated people, being forced to embark on a possibly deadly, many-month-long journey and to work for no pay far away from home and their families did not lead to a satisfied population.

The first few years for the European settlement were difficult. Constant internal and external rebellions, combined with the spreading of diseases and the lack of food and water, took a toll on everyone, especially the governor. Arthur Phillip organized and controlled essentially everything, much of which he was left to figure out on his own since communication from Britain took a long time to reach the new settlement. He created the settlement's first laws, organized mapmaking land and sea journeys, and took surveys to keep track of how the population was doing.

In 1790, only two years after the settlement's creation, Sydney was at its lowest point. Supplies were running out. Phillip did not really have an idea when supplies would arrive, as the ships could take at least five to seven months, and that's if they didn't go off course or run into complications. As it turns out, the HMS *Guardian*, which was the ship that was supposed to bring the settlement its supplies, ran into an iceberg and would never reach Australia. In the summer of 1790, a ship did arrive, carrying limited supplies that were meant to help support the hundreds of additional prisoners on the ship. However, since most of the convicts on the fleet were sick and did not require as much food, especially because so many had died, the supplies ended up helping the colony make it through this rough patch.

In 1791, the third fleet of prisoners arrived, which only helped to further cripple the already struggling colony. By 1792, the colony would finally begin to stabilize, yet, ironically, Arthur Phillip was in a poor state. His health was deteriorating, and he was sent home to England in order to recover. While he would not return to Australia, he would continue to sail as an admiral for the navy.

Governor John Hunter and the Arrival of Free Settlers (September 1795 to September 1800)

After Phillip returned to England, the colony was put in the control of Major Francis Grose and then Captain William Paterson while it was being decided who the next assigned governor would be. John Hunter, who was actually the second captain under Arthur Phillip of the original expedition to Australia, was chosen. In 1795, he returned to Australia.

Since the settlement was under military rule between the terms of Phillip and Hunter, it was not an easy transition for a new governor to take over, especially because the government that had been established in New South Wales was inefficient and sometimes unprofessional. An example of this can be seen in the communication with the duke of Portland, who was the governor liaison to the king. The duke of Portland would hear information from various settlers rather than one formal update. He would communicate with the king about the information he heard and send back instructions to the governor. The information came from many sources, and it must be remembered that many were unsatisfied with the harsh life in the first few years in Sydney. Since the correspondence was being taken as fact despite being opinions, the king did not truly know what was occurring in the colony, and the governor rarely received applicable instructions.

To make matters more complicated, at the time of Hunter's return, New South Wales had a population of 3,211, of which nearly 60 percent were prisoners. This, of course, made it difficult to introduce a non-military government, as the convicts had to be kept in line to ensure they followed through on their sentence.

While the colony had discovered how to grow its own grain, it was otherwise completely dependent on importing food, including cattle and sheep. Since an entirely new settlement was being constructed, little emphasis had actually been put on agriculture or economic activity. Much of the land had been used for government buildings and basic infrastructure. However, in the few months before and after John Hunter's arrival, this began to change, as farmers were beginning to look over their own plots.

Although there were many poorly executed elements to the government, upon arriving in New South Wales, Hunter decided to forgo many of his instructions that did not seem applicable to the colony's situation. For example, Hunter was told to introduce policies that would harm local farmers but would increase profits for Britain. Once arriving in New South Wales, Hunter realized that the colony needed to invest time and energy into producing food to sufficiently feed themselves before being able to send products to earn profits for Britain. He decided to encourage local farmers, a move that had been started by his predecessors.

Despite the fact that John Hunter was the governor, the colony struggled to transition to its new leadership. Much of the power remained in the hands of the military. One of the more profitable products at the turn of the century was rum, which was completely controlled by the soldiers. The rum industry quickly became corrupted, as did many sectors of the colony's economy and government. The population had trouble trusting the government, even when it transitioned to its new leadership because the untrustworthy military still remained a large part of the government. Despite all of this, John Hunter persevered and remained passionate in advancing the colony and Britain's understanding of Australia. His early efforts, as well as the work put in by Phillip and the in-between governors, helped to stabilize the situation in the first European Australian settlement.

Once the spread of illness and the food situation had somewhat stabilized in Sydney, the first free settlers (those not working for the prison system, in charge of the colony, or working on exploring the land) began arriving at the settlement. In 1793, two years before John Hunter returned to Australia to govern New South Wales, two British families as well as five freemen arrived in the colony. The British government began encouraging free citizens to immigrate to Sydney, and it offered the convicts as a labor force that could help new settlers build up their own businesses abroad. Those who showed promise of being able to grow Sydney's economy were actually assigned convicts in order to make their work easier. It wouldn't be until over twenty years later that the immigration of free settlers would really pick up.

Over the next few decades, fleets of prisoners would continue to be shipped to Australia, as the British jails were still overcrowded. Seeing that most of the convicts abroad were convicted of small crimes and only sentenced to a few years, between the 1790s and the 1810s, most of the original prisoners were either almost finished with their sentences or freemen. Most of the ex-convicts would go on to become tradesmen and laborers, as many were needed to build housing and infrastructure in the growing settlement. However, some ex-convicts managed to become successful, either by pursuing a skill, starting a business, or acquiring and farming a plot of land. Some of the more notable ex-convicts in Sydney include the painter Thomas Watling, Australia's first novelist Henry Savery, iconic architect Francis Greenway (he was actually on the country's $10 note for some time), and landowner and merchant Samuel Terry, who was one of the settlement's richest people. Although many convicts went on to find some form of stability and small success, and even though many were only convicted for small crimes, for over a century, it was seen as extremely negative to be related to ex-convicts.

Ironically enough, the penal settlement was still being controlled by a group of corrupt leaders, specifically the military. When John Hunter had first visited New South Wales alongside Arthur Phillip, the colony was entirely in the hands of the governor. He controlled everything from the land grants and labor allocation to the military and food supplies. However, when John Hunter returned to become governor of the colony, the military had completely taken over all of those aspects, leaving the governor with little power.

While John Hunter had good intentions and managed to advance the colony during his short stint as governor, he had trouble imposing his policies. In 1799, after approximately four years as governor, the military began sending falsified reports of Hunter's incompetence to Lord Sydney and the British authorities. By the end of the year, John Hunter was recalled as governor, and in 1800, he returned to England, his reputation ruined. In 1802, Hunter published "Governor

Hunter's Remarks on the Causes of the Colonial Expense of the Establishment of New South Wales. Hints for the Reduction of Such Expense and for Reforming the Prevailing Abuses," which helped to inform the British government and royal family of what was truly going on in Australia. This helped to restore his reputation.

Governor Philip Gidley King (September 1800 to August 1806)

In 1800, John Hunter was replaced as governor by Philip Gidley King, who was actually Hunter's second lieutenant on the initial journey to New South Wales. Similar to his predecessor, King had actually returned home from Australia before returning to take the post as governor. Another thing King had in common with Hunter was his difficulties in dealing with the military, which did not make it easy for the governor to impose new policies. Despite these conflicts, Philip Gidley King managed to help the colony develop in a positive direction at the expense of his own health, relationships, and reputation. King would return to England, once again sickly. He gave up his governorship in 1806.

The colony made many advancements during King's governorship, including new discoveries and settlements. During his predecessor's time in office, settlements had been made around New South Wales and one on Norfolk Island. However, with the discovery of the Bass Strait, King was really able to focus on colonizing southern Australia and the island of Tasmania. In 1803, David Collins formed a small settlement in Port Phillip, which is located just south of modern-day Melbourne, which is Australia's second-largest city after Sydney. In 1803, John Bowen led settlers to southern Tasmania, and they formed a settlement at the Derwent River. In 1804, Collins resettled in Hobart, which is now the most populated city in Tasmania. A settlement was also formed in 1804 in northern Tasmania.

While settlements were being formed by other explorers under the instruction of the governor, Philip Gidley King himself was focusing on improving the living and working conditions in New South Wales and the new settlements. Over his six years as governor, King made great strides in improving employment conditions for both freemen and ex-convicts by improving wages, working hours, and safety. King encouraged the advancement of the economy and infrastructure. Under his command, convicts built up the settlements, adding more homes, barracks, bridges, and wharves. The production of animal products increased since more herds and flocks were imported for both consumption and labor. Other aspects of agriculture were also advanced, as King encouraged experiments with various products that led to the production of tobacco, hemp, indigo, and cotton. Under his leadership, the settlements began coal mining and hunting whales and seals, which produced skins and oils. These were in great demand.

King also began establishing schools that advanced the skills of tradesmen and aided convicts in transitioning into work after the end of their sentence. Vaccinations for smallpox were spread throughout the colony, and King aided in the establishment of the first newspaper, *The Sydney Gazette*, which began printing in 1803.

During the course of King's governorship, he actually began a relationship with a convict on Norfolk Island. This relationship would result in two sons, who would be sent to England to study. This may have inspired his policies toward improving the education of Australia and the quality of work and life for the convicts.

Despite attempting to keep good relations with the Aboriginal population, his encouragement of exploring and settling new areas led to hostility and violence between the old and new inhabitants of the land. Here lies the great paradox of Australia's history. Great advancements for the British colonies typically led to awful outcomes for the native population. While King was not as purposefully aggressive toward the Aborigines, his actions had consequences that were not truly understood by the non-native population until many years later.

According to Henry Reynolds, the author of *Forgotten War*, "During the first half of the 20th century the Aborigines were written out of Australian history. This had the convenient effect of hiding much of the domestic bloodshed, allowing the celebration of what came to be viewed as a uniquely peaceful history of settlement." For generations, it was taught that the governors kept peace with their neighbors, to the best of their ability, of course. However, the reports of harmony in the 18th and 19th centuries are not to be trusted. While it is hard to ascertain exactly how badly European settlement affected these early populations, as reports and censuses were skewed in order to make the British settlers look better, it is certain that the massive decrease in the Aboriginal population was not random or accidental. There is little information about the relations between the indigenous population and the settlers during the time of Philip Gidley King. However, we can assume that the formation of any new settlements did not impact the Aboriginal population in a positive way.

Governor William Bligh (August 1806 to January 1808)

After Philip Gidley King returned to England due to poor health, his position was filled by William Bligh. Bligh had actually sailed alongside James Cook on his last voyage to the Pacific and then spent his years commanding merchant ships. During his time at sea, Bligh had earned a reputation of being aggressive, which had gotten him into trouble, notably when a falling out with his first mate led to a large mutiny. Nonetheless, William Bligh was considered to be a strong leader. In 1806, he was chosen to replace King as the governor in New South Wales. While the position was a great honor, it was not a sought-after job considering life in the colony was so difficult. The previous two governors had actually fallen sick.

Bligh immediately began attempting to improve the colony by repairing buildings and putting an end to free land grants. This encouraged the British government to enforce the purchase of land, which would improve Australia's economic situation. However, much like his predecessors, Bligh would not truly be able to focus on introducing new policies since he had to deal with the New South Wales Corps, which continued to corrupt the economy and control the government. The New South Wales Corps, which was established in 1789, controlled the trade of rum, which had become currency within the settlements. The corps would pay farmers with rum for their products and then expect higher monetary payment for necessities, such as sugar, clothing, shoes, and tea, the trade of which was controlled by the corps. Of course, since the farmers were paid in rum by the corps, they struggled to afford basic necessities.

William Bligh quickly attempted to establish government stores and trading centers, redirecting shady exchanges between farmers and the corps to a controlled environment. The governor also attempted to promote the usage of British currency rather than rum. Furthermore, Bligh dissuaded the use of convicts for private corps usage and instead reassigned them to public work, such as government farming and construction. This way, the corps could not profit unfairly off of free or cheap labor. To diminish the power of the corps further, Bligh destroyed houses that were built illegally by the corps. The most notable was the demolition of the home of John Macarthur, who was a leader in the New South Wales Corps.

All of the aforementioned actions led to massive conflicts with the corps, and Bligh was considered to be a tyrant. While these changes certainly helped to reduce the amount of power that the New South Wales Corps had over the colony, the situation worsened for William Bligh. The corps continuously demanded that Bligh ease up on his policies, and when he refused, the conflict reached its height. In 1808, the military stormed the governor's house. Major George Johnston, Bligh's military officer, placed the governor under arrest. This revolt came to be known as the Rum Rebellion. William Bligh remained as a prisoner of the New South Wales Corps for a year, although he had some liberties. His successor, Lieutenant Colonel Lachlan Macquarie, sent him home to England.

Historically, Bligh is viewed as a somewhat controversial leader. Although he made great strides for the colony during his short term, he was seen as cruel, even before he took up the governorship. Historians are unsure as to the accuracy of the reports of his leadership, as even farmers and convicts were unable to be truthful due to pressure from the military.

Chapter 5 – Land Expansion and Significant Political, Social, and Judiciary Developments for the Colonies (1810 to 1831)

Governor Lachlan Macquarie (January 1810 to November 1821)

Between 1808 and 1810, the colony was once again under the control of the New South Wales Corps, which maintained a military rule over the settlements. It continued its corrupt practices, which took a toll on the other members of Australia's society. Although the military leadership was supposed to end as soon as it began, the original choice for governor fell sick. In 1810, Lieutenant Governor Lachlan Macquarie was forced to step into the position. While many of his predecessors achieved great strides for the colony, Macquarie is considered to have been the most consequential of the early governors.

Immediately upon his arrival in New South Wales, Macquarie noticed the state of the hospital, which was essentially a grouping of poorly constructed buildings and tents. It was nowhere near the necessary standard for the growing colony, which had grown to over twenty thousand settlers. Macquarie decided one of his first tasks as governor would be to construct a new hospital. He promptly set aside land and requested permission from the British government. The proposal was denied, but Macquarie was not giving up easily. Since he could not receive funding from the government, he requested aid from businessmen, namely Garnham Blaxcell, Alexander Riley, and D'Arcy Wentworth, who agreed to fund the project. In exchange, the businessmen would acquire a monopoly on rum profits, specifically the profits of up to forty-five thousand gallons of imported rum. This amount was eventually increased to sixty thousand gallons. The businessmen were also to earn a return on their investment for the construction of the hospital, as the use of convict labor lowered the cost of construction. There was now one central hospital, which was connected to two wings used as living quarters by the surgeons. While the final hospital was certainly a step up from the previous collection of crumbling structures and tents, it was not perfect, as many money- and time-saving approaches were implemented during construction.

After the hospital had been completed, Francis Greenway, an ex-convict who was Australia's first government architect, examined the building and claimed it was poorly constructed and that it would not last. According to accounts, Greenway actually said that the new hospital "must soon fall into ruin." After Greenway's report, Macquarie instructed the workers to fix some of the flaws in the construction. However, many would not be rectified until the late 20th century. Assuming Greenway's claims were correct, the changes implemented to the construction after his report must have made a difference, as the central hospital building remained standing until 1894, which was when it was replaced. The original wings, which had been renovated over the years, still stand and have been transformed for various purposes, including housing government officials. The south wing was once the Sydney Mint, but it is now a museum. D'Arcy Wentworth, who had been one of the businessmen and contractors who helped fund the building of the hospital, became the first surgeon in the new hospital.

Similar to his predecessors, Lachlan Macquarie focused much of his attention on development, both of the original New South Wales settlement and of new settlements throughout Australia. Macquarie strongly supported exploration, which led to the discovery of the Blue Mountains. This was a massive revelation, as the land in the Blue Mountains is much richer and more fertile than where the original New South Wales settlement had been constructed. Finding a route through the Blue Mountains, which is part of the Great Dividing Range, was no easy task since it had many natural obstacles, including dense bushes, predatory animals and pests, deep gorges, and labyrinths composed of sandstone cliffs. That being said, two men, William Lawson and William Charles Wentworth, managed to make it through there alive in 1813 by traveling along the ridges rather than through the valleys. The latter of the mentioned explorers was actually the son of the hospital's first surgeon.

The following year, Macquarie ordered William Cox, a road builder, to organize the construction of a road through the Great Dividing Range. Of course, while this expansion toward Australia's interior was phenomenal for the European settlement, it came at a cost. There had been many tribes of Aboriginal people living throughout and beyond the Blue Mountains. The most notably affected by the expansion was the Wiradjuri population, which lived around modern-day Bathurst.

While reports from the time detail peace between the settlers and the Aboriginals, it is difficult to tell whether these claims are true or not. According to journals written by Lachlan Macquarie himself, the Aborigines of that region displayed "fear at seeing so many strangers." Whether or not that was the extent of the settler and Aboriginal relationship during this period cannot be said for sure. However, the situation would only become more hostile and deadly in the next decades.

Meanwhile, as construction began to impose more and more on the land of the Aborigines, Lachlan Macquarie encouraged the development of New South Wales, specifically the Sydney settlement. Planning began as soon as Macquarie arrived in Australia, and within a decade of being governor, over two hundred different public buildings had been constructed, including barracks, courthouses, churches, schools, banks, and parks. Most of this infrastructure had not yet existed in the Australian settlements until his arrival. For example, Macquarie established the colony's first bank in 1817. A few years prior, in 1813, he had instituted the colony's own currency; until that point, British currency and rum were used. Many of these buildings, some of which still stand today, were actually designed by ex-convict Francis Greenway. Two of his iconic designs from this period, which remain standing on Macquarie Street, are the Hyde Park Barracks and St. James Church.

On top of encouraging the construction of infrastructure, Lachlan Macquarie supported the development and expansion of agriculture. Much of his plan relied on emancipist agriculture or, in other words, farming by ex-convicts. That being said, it wasn't only the ex-convicts who were farming. During the course of Macquarie's governorship, Sydney was transformed from a home mainly for current and ex-convicts into a decent city that attracted the attention of free Europeans.

Gradually, advancements, specifically those by Governor Macquarie as well as John Macarthur, made in Australian agriculture and the New South Wales economy reached Britain. Macarthur, who actually had his illegally-constructed home destroyed by former Governor William Bligh, was a member of the New South Wales Corps and a landowner. He made great strides in agriculture for the settlement. By 1815, John Macarthur and other pastoralists had demonstrated the economic potential of farming animals for both meat and wool, and immigration began picking up. The British government reinstated their promotions, which encouraged citizens to immigrate to the Australian settlements. New settlers were offered plenty of ex-convict laborers, and by the 1820s, men began arriving in larger numbers to get their start in Australia's booming pastoral industry.

The arrival of immigrants brought rapid growth to the colony's economy. Despite the growth of the pastoral industry, during the 1810s until the 1830s, the primary exports would be from fishing and the hunting of marine animals, mainly whales and seals. That being said, the pastoral industry gradually picked up momentum. By 1834, the exportation of wool and other products would overtake the previous primary sources of income. Eventually, the population was no longer made up of a majority of convicts. Instead, it was composed of free people and emancipists, which required a change in the governmental and political organization.

At the beginning of Macquarie's governorship, the New South Wales Corps not only dominated the economy but also controlled the court. As more free settlers arrived in New South Wales, the population became mostly split between those who supported the military control enforced by the corps and those who didn't. Regardless of how the population was split, the military rule was no longer working. Neither was the governor's authoritarian rule, which had been instituted at the birth of the New South Wales settlement. In 1814, Macquarie introduced a new Charter of Justice for New South Wales, which reorganized the civil court system into three sections. These three civil courts were separated into the Governor's Court, the Lieutenant Governor's Court, and the Supreme Court.

Although Macquarie had organized the new civil court system, he had little say as to who served on the court. Soon after introducing the Charter of Justice for New South Wales, Lord Bathurst sent over Ellis Bent and his brother Jeffery Hart Bent to act, respectively, as the judge advocate and the judge of the Supreme Court. Unfortunately, the Bent brothers and Governor Macquarie disagreed on most topics from the very beginning. Their hostile relationship was not helped by the fact that the Bent brothers quickly allied themselves with the New South Wales Corps upon their arrival.

One example of the many disagreements between Macquarie and Ellis and Jeffery Hart Bent was on the topic of emancipists, which had already been a controversial topic in the colony. The corps had long since held the belief that opportunities should be given exclusively to settlers rather than ex-convicts. Even before the arrival of the Bents, the corps had strongly disagreed on Macquarie's agricultural developments, which relied on emancipist farming. They also disagreed on who could practice law in the New South Wales courts. Governor Lachlan Macquarie strongly believed that the courts should allow emancipist attorneys. However, since Jeffery Bent was the judge of the Supreme Court and since his views aligned with those of the corps, this request was swiftly denied.

Almost a year after the introduction of the new charter, Frederick Garling and William Moore arrived from London. They were prepared to not only act as attorneys but also ensure that British law was followed in these faraway colonial courts. The British government ordered that the laws introduced in New South Wales had to be consistent with those of the British courts. This led to a lot of conflicts, as it was always debated whether or not the governor and attorneys were keeping in line with the laws. In addition, Macquarie was often reported as not staying consistent with British law. The Bent brothers, along with other members of the corps who remained within the court, often sent complaints to the British government, claiming that Macquarie was not following the newly imposed charters and instead acted as an authoritarian. In 1819, the British government, aided by John Macarthur, began investigating these claims against the governor. In 1821, Macquarie was recalled, putting an end to his governorship.

Governor Thomas Makdougall Brisbane (December 1821 to December 1825)

Land Grants and Consolidation

Thomas Makdougall Brisbane arrived in New South Wales in November of 1821 and officially took over the governor position on

December 1st. Before moving to Australia, he served in the British army and practiced and invested in the advancement of astronomy. Upon his arrival, the main pressing issue that had to be dealt with was that of the promised land grants. Over 340,000 acres of land grants had been promised without the actual space or prepared location. To make matters worse, land was mostly transferred illegally or informally at this time, which made it difficult to keep track of what land was owned and what was available.

Within the first few months of his arrival, Brisbane introduced a new system of passing out tickets of leave, assigning land to some of those with promised grants. Only those who planned to use the assigned land productively were given tickets of leave, and surveyors were hired in order to track debts. Land was assigned to immigrants according to their wealth. Much land was also given to those born in Australia whose fathers had improved their property. Brisbane encouraged the immigration of those who could afford to use their land productively. He introduced laws that forced those with tickets of leave to have at least one convict working on every one hundred acres of their farm at all times. Since land was limited at this time, in order to cut down on the number of tickets of leave given out, Brisbane introduced various policies that would restrict many from receiving these land grants. One of these laws stated, "Every person to whom a grant is made receives it as the payment of a debt; everyone to whom one is refused turns into my implacable enemy." In order to further cut down on the discrepancy of land granted in regards to available land, Brisbane requested that the British government offer less acreage in every land grant.

Unlike Brisbane's predecessors, he put little effort into exploration. He instead focused on surveying and consolidating the land already within the colony. As already known by Brisbane, there was not enough land to meet the number of free grants being given out. John Thomas Bigge, who was actually the commissioner sent to New South Wales by Lord Bathurst to investigate the actions of Lachlan

Macquarie, remained involved in politics. He generally seemed to agree with Brisbane's decisions as governor. Bigge suggested that New South Wales should sell Crown land for 5 shillings an acre. Bigge felt that the colony would always be lacking in land to meet all of the land grants until landowners began paying for their land; this suggestion was enacted in 1824. A quote from John Bigge explains his reasoning: "While the system of free grants exists, there is little chance of extensive improvement taking place generally in the colony, as the improver of land can never enter the market in competition with the individual who gets his land for nothing." Within a few months after the policy was formally enacted, New South Wales sold over 500,000 acres of land.

Agricultural Advancements

As mentioned previously, Brisbane made it much harder for settlers to obtain land, withdrawing many of the programs and assistance that allowed those without much capital to afford land. That being said, he did not want to put an end to agricultural expansion and development. In 1822, he founded and joined the New South Wales Agricultural Society. Around the same time, he set up an agricultural training college. The New South Wales Agricultural Society aided in financing imports and experiments, most of which turned out to be unsuccessful.

The Division of Political and Judicial Responsibilities

Meanwhile, in order to not repeat what had occurred with the previous governor, Brisbane was in constant communication with Bigge and Lord Bathurst, who were mostly focused on convict affairs. Although Macquarie had achieved great strides for the colony, his reputation was somewhat controversial, as he was seen as being too lenient with the convicts and independent since he did not listen to the British government's advice. Brisbane apparently put an unofficial ban on offering convicts early tickets of leave, which was a common practice in the colony at the time. In order to kill two birds with one stone, Brisbane gathered up convicts who were still involved in criminal activities and those working on public construction projects and had them work together to clear land. This helped to reduce crime, give jobs to convicts, and create land for land grants and room for new settlers. Convicts with skills were hired for work that counted toward their sentence rather than being assigned to random public work, which helped to fill the gaps in various industries.

Under the guidance of Bigge and Lord Bathurst, Governor Brisbane opened more centers of secondary punishment for reoffending prisoners or those who needed to be in a higher security facility. The two centers of secondary punishment opened by Brisbane were in the Moreton Bay region and on Norfolk Island. The latter was where one of the original settlements had actually been established and then abandoned. Although Brisbane was certainly stricter when it came to convict affairs than the previous governors, he was still considered to be tame compared to what was expected of him by the British government. For example, he pardoned many death sentences, as he did not believe in excessive punishment.

By the time of Brisbane's governorship, what had been done by his predecessors was no longer possible. The colony had grown, and one man could not run it alone. Brisbane was known to take advice from many and not only Bigge and Bathurst. He took financial advice from Colonial Secretary Frederick Goulburn and Deputy Commissary General William Wemyss. When Goulburn and Wemyss advised that Brisbane should reform the colony's currency, he did so. More than ever before, work was handed off to lower levels of administration; in the case of Brisbane, he gave it to his lieutenant governors, William Sorell and George Arthur.

Further work was accomplished to break down the work in the courts. In New South Wales, between 1823 and 1828, various acts were introduced that divided the courts into Executive and Legislative Councils. These included both nominated private individuals and officers of the government. Since Tasmania was still under the domain of the governor of New South Wales, Brisbane also helped to create the Supreme Court of Tasmania in 1824, which helped to further divide his responsibilities. These decisions to take the advice of others and reduce his own responsibilities and, therefore, his power made Governor Thomas Makdougall Brisbane somewhat controversial, ironically for the complete opposite reasons than his predecessor. Many found Brisbane to be not only weak and susceptible to persuasion but also an inefficient and poor administrator.

Brisbane's Legacy

Regardless of what others said about him, Brisbane's choice to pass off some of the responsibilities was overall beneficial since it allowed him to pursue some of his other passions, even while acting as governor. For example, Brisbane had passionately studied astronomy before immigrating to New South Wales. In 1822, he constructed an observatory at Parramatta, which is a suburb of modern-day Sydney. This new infrastructure allowed Brisbane to make some of the first astronomical reports in the Southern Hemisphere. Brisbane was so dedicated to furthering science in the colony that when his governorship ended, he left all of his equipment and most of his books behind. He also left behind the city of Brisbane. It began in 1824 as a convict settlement like many of the settlements in Australia, but today, it is the capital of Queensland, Australia.

William Charles Wentworth

Brisbane was not the only one making advancements for New South Wales. William Charles Wentworth, who became a public figure after being one of the first Europeans to cross the Blue Mountains, influenced the future of the colony, debatably just as much as the governor. In 1819, he published a book describing the history and politics of New South Wales and Van Diemen's Land (Tasmania). His work had great political ramifications. It inspired a more liberal administration and would eventually lead to the New South Wales Constitution of 1855.

In 1824, Wentworth established *The Australian*, a newspaper that outwardly opposed the government and instead encouraged the creation of a representative government. *The Australian* also pushed for better conditions for emancipists, a belief that William Wentworth likely inherited from his father, considering his wife, William's mother, was an ex-convict. Ten years after its creation, *The Australian* would be used to push Wentworth's political party, the Australian Patriotic Association. Regardless of the fact that *The Australian* was not supportive of Brisbane's government or its policies toward emancipists, Brisbane did not censor the newspaper. Brisbane also put an end to military and government control of the *Gazette* and other institutions that had been censored for years.

Brisbane's Recall

As previously mentioned, Brisbane split up his responsibilities and sought advice from multitudes of people within his administration. While most of his advisors were trustworthy, others were more controversial, which led Brisbane to get into some trouble. One of the men from whom Brisbane sought advice was Dr. Henry Grattan Douglass, a doctor who had worked at the new hospital and opened up his own private practice in New South Wales. Douglass was a problematic alliance for Brisbane, as he had been in trouble with the British War Office. On top of continuing to employ and support Douglass, which was a controversial course of action, Brisbane had many issues with Frederick Goulburn, the colonial secretary. Goulburn disagreed with some of Brisbane's policies and often hid information, rejected his superior's ideas, and responded to important letters meant for Brisbane, impersonating the governor. By 1824, Goulburn began claiming more power for himself by redirecting political reports from the governor, claiming they had to go through his department before they reached the population. Brisbane attempted to complain to the Colonial Office. However, Britain had reached its limit and decided to just recall both Brisbane and

Goulburn. At the end of 1825, the governor officially left the colony to return home to England.

Governor Ralph Darling (December 1825 to October 1831)

Following the recall of Thomas Brisbane, Britain sent Ralph Darling to replace him as governor. Before arriving in New South Wales, Darling was a military general, and he had some experience in political administration since he had been a governor in Mauritius. New South Wales and its dependencies, both of which were gradually growing larger, were put in the hands of Darling in mid-December 1825. Around the time of Darling's arrival, New South Wales had expanded to include Bathurst and Melville Islands.

Darling was determined not to make a similar mistake as his predecessor by trusting the wrong people, so his strategy was to only involve people in politics that he could completely trust. He invited his brothers-in-law, Henry and William Dumaresq, to act, respectively, as his private secretary and civil engineer. He made William's father-in-law, Alexander Macleay, his colonial secretary, and a few years after his arrival, he assigned the position of assistant private secretary to Charles Darling, his nephew. Otherwise, Darling listened to the king and his officials, to whom he was fiercely loyal.

Political Reforms

Since there had been so many issues with the previous governors, Darling was instructed to ask for advice and make decisions with the Executive Council, which included the lieutenant governor, chief justice, colonial secretary, and the archdeacon. A Legislative Council was also formed for this reason; however, Darling was able to nominate the members of this council. To ensure that Darling would not lead as an authoritarian or go against the instructions of the British government, Darling was forced to submit reports and explanations for every decision or act that had been established without the consultation of the councils. Unsurprisingly, with his military background, Ralph Darling focused on efficiency and did not care for the disorganized political, public, or economic systems that had been established by his predecessors.

During Darling's governorship, many of the systems previously enacted were no longer working. Acts were also expiring, which led to the necessity of political reforms. These were of great debate to just about everyone involved. While many supported the creation of a house of assembly, Darling did not, as he believed the elected body could easily be immoral and make poor decisions for the colony. Darling's opinion was echoed by many, and he instead suggested that the colony's Legislative Council be expanded.

These debates sparked a sort of rivalry between Governor Ralph Darling and New South Wales Chief Justice Francis Forbes. While the two had gotten along before the conversations of political reform, which began around 1827, Forbes believed that Darling was attempting to keep more power for himself and that he was encroaching into what was supposed to be judiciary power. Forbes quite passionately believed that the political and judicial organizations would be bettered by enlarging the councils, which would help strengthen the system. In 1828, a new act was introduced that took into account both of the men's opinions. As advised by Darling, the Legislative Council grew to fourteen members, and as suggested by Forbes, seven of the fourteen members were elected and non-official.

After the Act of 1828, the governor not only had to discuss all decisions with the councils, including the creation of smaller bills, but members could also now introduce their own bills for discussion. Bills would only be enacted if the majority agreed. Another change to the councils was that what was discussed was no longer private, and all bills were to be submitted to the press to be published for the public to read. Even after being enacted, any bills could be submitted for review to the courts, and the judges had the opportunity to challenge its existence, especially if it did not remain consistent with the British courts.

Despite considering various opinions, many in New South Wales were unsatisfied with the political reforms since they did not change anything. The Executive Council had not been altered in any way, which meant that Darling still held much of the executive control in an authoritarian manner. On top of this, the Legislative Council was mostly made up of Darling's allied government officials and "exclusives," a term used to describe the wealthy people in the colony. This meant that the changes made to the Legislative Council did little to strengthen the decisions of the colony as Forbes had intended; instead, it only strengthened Darling's power.

The Legislative Council almost entirely maintained similar beliefs on the matter of ex-convicts, which was massively debated in the colony, considering it was occupied by emancipists. The Legislative Council mostly agreed that ex-convicts could not be trusted and should not have the same opportunities as free members of society. This, of course, put him at odds with the liberal citizens, such as William Charles Wentworth and Robert Wardell, who wrote negatively about their governor in the newspapers.

After arriving in New South Wales, Ralph Darling was instructed to assign convicts who had proven they could reform to settlers, who would then put them to work. Convicts who did not seem to be capable of reforming were sent to harsher penal settlements, which were being constructed all over the colony. While Darling did not follow these instructions exactly, he did employ convicts who seemed to be incorrigible on jobs with harsh conditions. Many convicts who were deemed incapable of reforming were sent to chain gangs to work in inhumane conditions. But it seemed that after separating the convicts into those who were capable and not capable of reforming, there were not enough convicts who could be assigned to the growing number of settlers. An Assignment Board was created to aid the placing of convicts. However, it would seem that most disagreed with Darling's decisions, including those who supported the rights of the convicts and those who agreed with Darling that the convicts and even ex-convicts should not be considered as equal to the freemen.

Another example of how the political reforms did little to challenge Darling's power was the changes made to land distribution, grants, and division. Although Darling's predecessor had addressed these concerns, the colony was growing, both in convicts and in free people, which meant that the policies regarding these aforementioned matters needed to change. While there was the Australian Agricultural Company, which had good relations with the British, the members of the colonial government and Darling felt differently. Within the colony, it was known that the Australian Agricultural Company was not always trustworthy nor efficient and that fraud and absenteeism were prevalent in the distribution of land. Darling established the Land Board, which would take a closer look at who was receiving land grants and enforce that settlers earned grants proportionate to their capital. Land alienation, which is the transfer of land from one to another, was forbidden, as it was difficult to keep records of and promoted illegal trades. Darling also introduced land grants for daughters with dowries, widows, and government officials. He enacted all of these changes in land distribution with little conflict, as the Executive Council was made up of his closest allies.

Many in the colony felt as though his new policies in regards to land grants were actually regressing the colony and that his acts did little to reduce the discrepancy between land demands and available land. This only supported Forbes and the others who claimed Darling was acting with authoritarian power and not considering the betterment of the colony. Dissatisfaction with Darling was upheld by the Australian Agricultural Company, specifically T. L. Mitchell, its surveyor-general. Eventually, Darling stopped the sales of Crown lands entirely and granted further land to the Church and School Corporation, which went against the original instructions of the British government.

All that being said, Darling did make some good reforms in regards to land division and distribution, one of which was his decision to divide the colony into counties and parishes. His decisions ended up leading to the 1831 Ripon regulations, which brought about an entirely new system for the distribution of land in Australia.

Economic, Banking, and Monetary Reforms

At the time of Ralph Darling's arrival in New South Wales, the economy was in a slump, mostly because the British treasury had eliminated the colony's dollar currency, reducing the currency's worth. To make matters worse, New South Wales had been experiencing a drought for almost three years, which made agriculture even more difficult for the settling Europeans than it already was because of how much of a shift the climate and terrain was. The colony's banks had been requesting government loans in order to help with the financial troubles.

However, before giving them any money, Darling and his councils decided to take a deeper look into the banks' activities. It was discovered that many of the government's financial departments and the banks' administrators had been stuffing their own paychecks with government money that was meant to be used for the colony's betterment.

After reporting this to the British government, it was instructed that all government funds needed to be securely locked in a vault and regularly collected and counted. The banks were only to hold £10,000 maximum in order to prevent further corruption. Within a few years, the economy of New South Wales recovered, and as a direct consequence of Darling's decisions, the colony's funds doubled.

Explorations and Expansion

Unlike his predecessor, who focused mostly on consolidating the colony's land, Ralph Darling reemphasized the importance of exploring and expanding the colony. Under Darling's governorship, explorer and botanist Allan Cunningham explored north of the colony, expanding the Europeans' understanding of the landscape and plant life throughout Australia all the way to New Zealand. Cunningham ended up spending most of his time exploring the Darling Downs and the Richmond River. Captain Charles Sturt traveled west and, between 1828 and 1830, traveled along the Murrumbidgee and Murray rivers.

Darling also encouraged the construction of roads, branching out in all directions from Sydney. In 1827, Captain James Stirling explored the Swan River located near the modern-day city of Perth on the western coast of Australia. In 1829, the colony of Swan River was formed; now, it is known as the state of Western Australia. Although they would turn out to be unsuccessful, Darling attempted to establish ports and settlements on the western coast.

Darling's Reputation and Recall

Similar to the other governors of the New South Wales colony, Ralph Darling was a controversial leader with many avid supporters and haters. Although popular opinion was mostly positive at first, within a few years, he had lost the public's favor. This was mostly due to his intense military beliefs and authoritarian approach. This dissatisfaction was fueled by William Charles Wentworth and Robert Wardell, who used their newspapers to analyze all the governor's decisions. Darling was not only displeased with what was being published, but he also felt that he was being misrepresented in the press and that "exaggerations and lies were being published." In 1827, Darling requested the establishment of the Newspaper Regulating Act, which was allowed. After Edward Smith Hall of *The Monitor* was jailed and *The Australian*'s editor was fined for publishing attacks in the newspaper, the Newspaper Regulating Act was amended and intensified. Darling was greatly criticized for his decisions to repress free discussion.

However, all of that being said, none of this would be the reason for Ralph Darling's recall. After six years as governor, his assigned term had ended. And unlike his predecessors, who were specifically recalled for their actions, Darling simply ended his term and returned to England. Although Darling was heavily criticized and was certainly an intense leader, he managed to advance the colony in many ways. In his words, "General popularity is not always the companion of integrity...it would have been impossible to satisfy many of the [colonists] without an abandonment of every principle of justice and duty."

During Darling's governorship, the colony continued to accept nearly four thousand convicts per year. However, that being said, between the free settlers and the growing number of emancipists, the population of around seventy-five thousand people was only 50 percent convicts. The half of the population that was not currently convicted was mostly made up of ex-convicts, which the colony was still unsure how to handle. By 1830, close to sixty thousand convicts had been sentenced to the New South Wales penal settlements, many of whom, by this time, had worked off their sentence. Overall, the colony's demographics were changing, gradually developing from a penal settlement into a free colony, which meant that the administration, systems, and economy needed changes as well.

Of course, the growing population was not so positive for the Aborigines, with whom the colonists shared the land. As the colony needed more space to expand, the relationship with the native population, who had their land stolen, was only becoming more hostile. Nelson Lawson, one of the seven elected members of the Legislative Council and son to William Lawson, who had discovered the path across the Blue Mountains with William Charles Wentworth, was quoted in 1824 as saying, "We have now commenced hostilities against them [the Aboriginals] in consequence of their killing a great number of shepherds and stockmen, but afraid we shall never exterminate them, they have such an extensive mountainous country for them to flee from their pursuers." During Darling's governorship, the situation with the Aboriginals was already hostile, as described by Nelson Lawson. However, in the coming years, with the growing settler population and need for expansion, the situation was only going to worsen.

Chapter 6 – Liberal Administration and Self-Government (1831 to 1850)

Governor Richard Bourke (December 1831 to December 1837)

After the recall of Ralph Darling, Richard Bourke was called on to fill his spot. Similar to his predecessor, Bourke had served in the military and had experience acting as a governor. Bourke landed in New South Wales on December 3rd, 1831, and was immediately a controversial leader, even before taking over the governorship. While Bourke had an incredible reputation as a leader, he was a passionate Whig; in other words, he was a liberal. For half of the population, the emancipists, the convicts, and the liberals, this was a welcome change.

However, since Ralph Darling had been a Tory (a conservative), much of the administration and almost the entirety of the Legislative and Executive Councils was conservative. The executives of New South Wales, who were the elites of society, were almost all Tories as well, and their political affiliations made them immediately displeased with their new governor. Though Bourke had some powerful allies, including Chief Justice Francis Forbes, William Charles Wentworth

(*The Australian*'s founder), and a good percentage of the population itself, his list of powerful enemies was much larger.

Judiciary Reforms Related to the Emancipists

Upon Bourke's arrival, a matter that had to be dealt with was the expiration of the Jury Act, which stated that court cases should have a jury of members of the military when applicable. Bourke's plan was to extend the act but make a few changes, most notably that the jury should not be limited to those in the military but should also be extended to emancipists. Though judges seemed to back his proposal, the conservative "exclusives," who were not in support of giving emancipists any more power or rights than they had already been accorded, were, of course, not in favor.

A few months after arriving, the Jury Act was renewed; however, Bourke's proposal of including civil, non-military people on the jury was denied. The following year, in 1833, the matter was repurposed after a petition circulated with a few thousand signatures. Since the proposed amendments to the Jury Act were in line with the British courts, the Legislative Council passed the amendments but only for certain situations.

Bourke was no stranger to prejudice, as his last governorship had been in Cape, South Africa, where he founded equal court treatment, which was something not often offered to the black population. The same seemed to be the case for the emancipated population of New South Wales. Most of the British criminals who had been sentenced to do time in Australia had committed minor crimes, mostly non-violent ones. Yet, once they had served their sentence, they were treated like lower-class citizens who deserved to lag behind the free people and feel shame for the rest of their life. This prejudice went against Bourke's liberal beliefs, especially in cases where it was so obvious, like in the courts, where it seemed judges, juries, and magistrates were far from impartial. Though New South Wales was more liberal in cases of ex-convicts on trial, many of the smaller settlements and more distant colonies were able to be more open with their prejudice.

Richard Bourke called on his chief justice, Francis Forbes, to create a bill that would reduce the possibility of this prejudice coming out in criminal law. The bill, which took away some of the magistrates' ability to punish those on trial, was supported by many magistrates. It was passed by the council, but it was, of course, completely opposed by Bourke's enemies, who felt that the governor went too easy on the ex- and present convicts. Nonetheless, the bill was passed, and since the magistrates had plenty of control, convicts and ex-convicts on trial remained at a disadvantage. Similarly, penal systems remained harsh, and despite Bourke's beliefs, he did little to change the conditions for convicts.

All of this being said, in some cases, the intense, harsh conditions were fair, which was why changing policies related to convict and ex-convict criminal law was difficult. For example, in Hunter River, which had some of the more dangerous convicts, going easy on convicts or ex-convicts was not an option since leniency could lead to massive issues. Although it wouldn't be changed under Richard Bourke's governorship, the usage of convict labor was becoming somewhat controversial, as it was often compared to slavery. While Bourke would speak out about the working conditions of those serving sentences, little would be achieved in that domain either.

Other Judiciary Reforms

Similar to Chief Justice Francis Forbes, Bourke maintained the liberal belief that New South Wales should have a house of assembly or at least more electives on the councils. In 1833, Bourke proposed introducing more electives into government. However, New South Wales was just not ready for it yet, especially considering its unique situation of balancing its own beliefs, the majority emancipated population, and the laws of the British courts and government.

In 1837, the 1828 Act, which had already been renewed for a year since the courts were too preoccupied to consider drawing up new judiciary systems, was about to expire. Bourke suggested that the government be one-third nominated and two-thirds elected. While the population seemed to agree with his proposal, the decision was once again delayed for another year. The British government was called to make a decision on what should be done with the organization of the New South Wales government, and finally, it was decided that no changes should be made until convict transportation to Australia either lessened or stopped altogether. In 1842, a constitutional change similar to what Bourke had proposed would finally be approved. However, it came too late, as the colony had completely changed within those few years, and further changes needed to be made.

The Economy and Land Trade

Although the Australian settlement's economy was gradually improving over the past few decades and governors, Bourke's term would bring massive economic growth. Over the six years of Bourke's governorship, the colony's revenue almost tripled, and the revenue from exports more than doubled. Although most of the growth was from the exportation of new products and the growth of trading relations, a good portion of this increase in revenue was from land sales. The immigration of free settlers, which had first begun to pick up in the 1810s, was rapidly increasing during Bourke's governorship. Between 1830 and 1850, at least 100,000 free people traveled to Australia's European colonies, hoping to make a life. During Bourke's term as governor alone, the population of the Australian European colonies increased from fifty-one thousand to ninety-seven thousand.

In 1831, in response to the mass immigration, Britain finally decided that Australia's available land was in enough demand that it could no longer be handed out as grants. The land was sold when it was deemed "available" by the Crown; however, squatting on Crown land that had not yet been claimed or sold was common. Landowners whose herds were growing would often take their sheep and cattle to graze on unsold Crown land, which made it difficult for the government to sell the land adjacent to occupied land. Authorities had trouble enforcing boundaries, and yearly, tens of thousands of dollars were being lost due to unsold land. Squatters went to court to debate that, in Australia's arid climate, sheep and cattle needed more land in order to survive. Policies were gradually introduced to combat these issues, and over the course of Bourke's governorship, acres upon acres of land surrounding the settlements were sold to British immigrants looking to escape the harsh living and working conditions back home.

Since Australian land sales and product exports were contributing so much money to the economy of both New South Wales and Britain, the government began facilitating immigration to Australia. At first, assisted passage was introduced, which allowed immigrants to travel to Australia for free. However, the cost of their trip was essentially a loan that the settlers would have to pay back. In the second half of the 1830s, the government realized it was more profitable not to request a repayment of the loan, as it allowed settlers to build profitable businesses and purchase greater amounts of land. In 1836, the system was changed, giving immigrants entirely free travel to Australia, assuming they would purchase land on arrival.

Expansion and Relations with the Aboriginal Population

Of course, this growth in land demand, immigration, and expansion were not as positive for the indigenous population. Every time the population and land ownership in the colonies increased, those two numbers decreased for the Aboriginal people. The same went for the living conditions and available food. Although some of the Europeans shared positive, peaceful relationships with the Aboriginal population, the harmony never lasted long. For example, in the mid-1830s, some squatters who roamed the lands around Port Phillip and Tasmania had made treaties with the Aboriginal population since they were traversing on their land rather than Crown land. Of course, since the British government viewed all of Australia as its possession, it did not matter if the Aboriginal population approved of their squatting.

Bourke was instructed to quickly establish settlements in those regions in order to put an end to both the squatting and the Aboriginal-European peace, as the peace agreements made it harder for the settlers to expand into new lands. This explains why Port Phillip grew so quickly into one of the continent's largest cities. Port Phillip is now the base for many of the government's buildings in Melbourne. As new settlements were established, the Aboriginals' territory shrank, especially around the coasts, where both groups of people preferred to live. Within a few decades, warring between the Europeans and Aboriginals would see the deaths of thousands of settlers and tens of thousands of Aboriginals. Aboriginals who did not fight still had lower life expectancies than before British occupation, as European diseases continued to spread through the tribes. The Aboriginal displacement also led to food struggles.

The warring between the colonists and the Aboriginals, which began with the European settlement in Australia in 1788 and went on until the 20th century, was known as the Frontier Wars. One of the most violent wars in the Frontier Wars took place in Tasmania (also known as the Tasmanian War), which began in 1824 and continued for seven years, lasting into the beginning of Richard Bourke's governorship. Since the war began during one of the periods where New South Wales and its dependencies were under military rule, martial law was established, which allowed soldiers and settlers to be as violent to the Aboriginal population as they wanted without any consequences. The Tasmanian War reached its climax in 1830 when the European settlers formed lines of soldiers that slowly forced the Aboriginal population to retreat into the southeast of Tasmania. Aboriginals who did not comply by leaving their home were killed on the spot. According to the records, only one thousand Aborigines were killed in the Tasmanian War. However, historians assume the death toll is greater than what was recorded. Although the Aboriginal population of Tasmania still survives today, the Tasmanian War almost exterminated the native population of the island.

Similar warfare occurred during the formation of southern Australia. During the first few years of Bourke's governorship, both the British and colonial governments began planning to establish settlements in South Australia. In the summer of 1834, the South Australia Act was established, allowing exploration and settlement to officially begin. What propelled the creation of South Australia was the fact that it would be a free settlement. All the land would be sold to laborers who could transform the land for economic profit. The colony would officially be established in 1836, and it would be the only state in all of Australia never to receive convict transports. Adelaide, the capital of South Australia, was formed in 1837. Although the first years were tough, it soon began to thrive, partially due to the fact that its population was entirely free.

Religion and Education

Considering that England was Protestant, it's not surprising that they intended for their Australian colonies to be devout Protestants. However, from the very beginning of New South Wales, religious affiliations were more nuanced than that. At the time of the establishment of New South Wales, Ireland was under the control of England, and it would remain so until the 20th century. This meant that many of the initial convicts sent to Australia were actually of Irish descent. The proportion of Irish convicts to English convicts increased in the late 18th century when the Irish Catholics rebelled against the English Protestants. Many of those involved in the political and religious rebellions were sentenced to serve time in the newly formed penal colonies in Australia. In 1803, the first Catholic services were held in New South Wales, as the governor at the time felt that the Irish convicts might rebel if they were denied the right to practice their Catholic faith. This was a controversial choice; however, services began being held by convicted Catholic priest James Dixon, which did little to satisfy the Irish convicts, who felt they should not have been convicted in the first place. Catholic convicts commonly rebelled in the early years of the colony. The political prisoners felt their time was being wasted, time that could be spent liberating their home country of Ireland. Over the following years, Catholic rights would be repeatedly removed and granted.

Governor Richard Bourke was controversial for many reasons, partially for being a liberal but also for being Irish-born. Although Bourke spent most of his life in England, his Irish roots gave him insight and sympathy to religious causes that the previous governor had not had. Bourke was an Anglican himself, which combines some beliefs from both the Protestant and Catholic Churches. By the time of Bourke's arrival, nearly a fifth of the European population in Australia was Catholic, yet they had no consistent religious rights. In 1836, Bourke passed the Church Act, which, despite opposition from the "exclusives," was approved by the Legislative Council and the New South Wales government. The Church Act gave equitable funding to both the Protestant and Catholic churches based on the number of supporters. This meant that, though the majority of funding was still given to the Protestant churches, around a fifth of the religious funding was given to the Catholic churches. It would be a while before other religious denominations would be given funding, such as the Congregationalists and Presbyterians, whose populations were slowly growing. The Church Act also forced the Protestant churches to share some of their responsibilities with the Catholic churches, such as education for the colonies.

Schools had gradually been constructed as the settlements developed. However, since there was no larger education board and since education was controlled by the Protestant Church, some districts had no schools at all. In other districts, schools were run by smaller churches that were not overseen. There, education was mostly focused on religion rather than general learning. Richard Bourke decided that the education system needed to be reformed, with properly trained teachers, general programs of education, and a board to oversee the individual schools. The "exclusives" on the board, most of whom were devout Protestants, were displeased by this proposal, especially because the reforms in education were so heavily supported by the Catholics and liberals. Though Bourke invested much of his time into trying to create a better education system, little would change due to the intense opposition. Since one of his main drives to continue serving as governor after the end of his term was reforming education, his enthusiasm for maintaining the position decreased, as he realized it would be impossible to make any real changes to education with the current opinions of the councils.

Bourke's Resignation

Over the course of Richard Bourke's governorship, tensions with the "exclusives" only worsened. Conflicts with the colonial treasurer, C. D. Ridell, were especially intense, and eventually, Bourke removed Ridell from the Executive Council. Although Bourke was supposed to have the power to suspend those on the Executive Council, Riddell was reinstated by the British government, which led Bourke to consider resigning. Though the British government wanted Bourke to stay, as he had achieved great strides for the colony during his governorship, they did little to lessen his conflicts with Riddell or the "exclusives." Due to the trouble Bourke had experienced trying to pass his education reforms and the constant tensions with his administration, Bourke felt that if he remained, he would have to pass policies he did not believe in. He did not want to betray his principles and honor. In December of 1837, Bourke formally resigned, and in late January 1838, he left the colony to return home to England.

Governor George Gipps (October 1837 to August 1846)

Following the resignation of Richard Bourke, George Gipps, a veteran with administration experience from his time in the West Indies, was chosen to fill the position. Like his predecessor, Gipps was a Whig (a liberal). Although all of the governors of New South Wales had to contend with difficulties, Gipps started his governorship at an odd time, as the Australian settlements were slowly wanting complete freedom from their monarch. This meant that Gipps not only had to balance the instructions from the British government but also the demands of the colonial population and the colonial government, which usually contradicted each other. Despite being a liberal, Gipps was more enthusiastically welcomed by the "exclusives," as he displayed extreme respect for the opinions of all those in the administration. However, over the course of his governorship, as the demand for a representative government continued to rise, the conflicts between the "exclusives" and the governor, which had existed on and off for the past few decades, were reignited.

Political and Judiciary Reforms

Although the "exclusives" held powerful control of the administrative councils and courts since the decrease of the military's power, their self-interested, conservative British opinions were not shared amongst the colony's population. The majority of the population did not want to exist in a penal colony any longer; even those who were emancipated did not feel the cost of maintaining the convicts was fair. Furthermore, colonists did not agree with the use of the budget or the taxes they had to pay that were not for colonial purposes but for the British government to profit.

Slowly, the majority of the population wanted to distance themselves from the monarchy and transition to self-government. These beliefs were echoed by the newspapers, lower-level government workers, members of the courts, emancipists, and, most notably, Governor George Gipps. In 1842, the government of New South Wales was the first Australian colony to gain self-governance, as the Legislative Council was comprised of two-thirds elected members. This gave electees the majority vote over the "exclusives," who were nominated by the British government and the furthest from whom the population would choose to be on their council.

However, with the laws in place determining who was allowed to vote, over 60 percent of white adult males in the colony were still not allowed to vote, meaning that the electees still did not align with whom the population would have chosen. A clean record and land ownership or a certain amount of capital were necessary to vote, which means mostly wealthy landowners were voted to be on the council. Despite the population being mostly liberal, the council remained mostly conservative, and the members outwardly opposed most of the opinions of Gipps and the population.

To make matters even worse, those who had once been the most influential liberals had slowly developed more conservative opinions, including William Charles Wentworth. As Wentworth aged, he built up his riches and focused on acquiring land. Thus, he began losing some of his liberal beliefs. When the population began demanding that convict transportation to Australia should end, Wentworth found himself siding with the "exclusives," who believed that convict labor was necessary since it gave them cheap workers they could abuse. His opinions had strayed so greatly that even the newspaper he founded, *The* Australian, published in 1842, "Mr. Wentworth...was an influential man. His day is gone by. His opinion is worth nothing...Certainly he first taught the natives of this colony what liberty was, but he has betrayed them since and they have withdrawn their confidence from him."

Wentworth was not alone in his changing beliefs. The emancipists had been strictly liberal since the creation of the colony; however, the richest of the emancipists, especially those who had been free for decades, found themselves sharing more in common with the "exclusives" and rich landowners than the other ex-convicts. Wentworth, who had once posed the greatest opposition to the conservative governors, became one of the greatest enemies of the now liberal governor. Much of this hostility came from the fact that in 1840, Wentworth had attempted to purchase a good portion of New Zealand's South Island for far less than it was worth. Gipps was quoted as saying, "Mr. Wentworth asks me to lend a hand in perpetrating; the job, that is to say, of making to him a grant of twenty million acres at the rate of one thousand acres for a farthing." As these conflicts intensified, Governor George Gipps, in 1843, said, "There are about five or six men in the council who are personally my enemies."

Despite the fact that the flow of convicts was passionately supported by Wentworth, the "exclusives," the landowners, and many of the richer emancipists, the transport of prisoners was temporarily paused to the New South Wales colony in 1840. That being said, the transport of convicts continued to Norfolk Island and Tasmania.

Meanwhile, on a smaller scale, settlements outside of New South Wales wanted freedom from colonial and monarchical rule. Gradually, all the colonies would receive self-governance, and the settlements would be divided into more colonies with their own respective governments. For example, in 1840, New Zealand gained its own government, meaning it governed itself separately from New South Wales. In Port Phillip, however, settlers were still under the New South Wales government, despite being quite a distance away. Port Phillip settlers had different beliefs than the administration of New South Wales, specifically when it came to the transportation of convicts. In 1842, when the Legislative Council became two-thirds elected, Port Phillip was only represented by six seats, and the representatives had to travel nearly one thousand kilometers to attend meetings. Considering the councils met quite often, Port Phillip's representatives were not always able to attend. Despite all of this, the British government was hesitant to give any settlement more power, as the requests for self-governance and the distancing from British laws and beliefs grew.

Penal Reforms

The future of the penal system was under great debate during Gipps's governorship. In fact, many aspects of the system were under debate, including whether more convicts should be sent to Australia and how to deal with the convicts already serving their sentences. Alexander Maconochie, who was the governor of Norfolk Island, decided to experiment with the penal system. Maconochie had more modern beliefs on crime and punishment. He believed the goal of the penal system should not be to punish the convicts but rather that punishment should be used as a tool within the system to reform the convicts. He believed that forcing the prisoners to do intensive labor until their sentence was finished did not help reform them. In fact, it had the opposite effect, as it would harden the prisoners and turn them against the government. Maconochie believed that rather than doing work as punishment, working efficiently and conducting themselves properly should be marked on a point system, which eventually would lead to freedom. Essentially, Maconochie believed time and punishment could not reform, but rewarding those who actually acted civilized and worked their hardest could.

Although Maconochie wanted to use the system for all of the convicts, and even though Gipps supported Maconochie, Gipps did not actually believe it was a good idea to experiment on all of the prisoners. Maconochie began his mark system in 1840 with all of the newest convicts, despite his feelings that results would be more dramatic on a larger testing pool. Since the results would affect whether or not the system continued or not, these numbers really mattered. However, Maconochie's system did not last long, and before any real results could be displayed, he was removed by the British government, likely because his contract was up.

Land Reforms

Although every governor had attempted to make some changes to the distribution and division of land in the colonies, as more settlers arrived and the demand for products increased, new issues arose that required the entire rehaul of the previous governor's systems. When Gipps arrived, the topic of squatters was once again relevant. The primary economic export in the 1840s was wool, and most squatters at this time were sheep farmers who traveled onto Crown lands they did not own because their sheep needed grazing pastures to survive in the arid climate. Considering that the squatters were providing much of the colonial revenue, their demand for tenure had to be addressed promptly. The situation was made even more complicated by the fact that the Legislative Council, which was to make the decision on the squatters' request for tenure, was made up mostly of "exclusives" and landowners, both of which profited off of the squatters' grazing in Crown lands.

Wentworth, who after being elected to the council had taken a sort of leadership position, was one of the main defenders of squatters' rights, seeing as his land ownership had grown significantly. In addition, like the other landowners, he benefited greatly from the allowance of squatting. Gipps, like much of the population, believed that the Crown lands should stay under the government's control until they were sold or granted to landowners.

However, squatters would graze unused lands, reducing their value and making it difficult to sell to new citizens. According to a quote by Gipps in 1843, "The lands are the unquestionable property of the Crown, and they are held in trust by the government for the benefit of the people of the whole British Empire. The Crown has not simply the right of a landlord over them, but exercises that right under the obligation of a trustee." In other words, Gipps believed it should be up to the government to decide who receives land, as squatting was taking away from land sale revenue and making it difficult to fill the demand for land from new settlers.

Gipps decided the best way to meet everyone's demands was to introduce quitrents (a tax on the occupants of the land; it was essentially rent), which would force squatters to pay for the land they grazed on outside of their boundaries. By 1844, the squatters, who were already suffering due to droughts, were extremely dissatisfied with Gipps and threatened rebellion. Despite the opposition, Gipps continued to release extreme squatting policies, including one that forced squatters to repeatedly repurchase their land for eight-year terms.

Considering New South Wales was in a sort of financial depression at this time, these policies led to much of the population being dissatisfied with Gipps. The drought in Australia in the 1840s meant immigration had slowed down, and land was less in demand, leading many to question why Gipps did not wait to introduce these policies. Although Gipps's policies were more than fair, as they really only punished the richest landowners who were squatting on most of the Crown lands, the timing of his policies and the power of the squatters led to the ruin of Gipps's reputation.

Economy

As previously mentioned, during George Gipps's governorship, the economy was in disarray. This was mainly due to the drought, which not only reduced revenue on agricultural products (which made up a majority of the economic sector at this time) but also reduced the land demand from settlers, which contributed greatly to the colony's revenue. When Great Britain refused to loan money to the suffering colony, Gipps borrowed money from the military chest and then from colonial merchants, banks, and even the newspapers.

Immigration and Education

Although immigration had slowed down at some points during Gipps's governorship, it was mostly the immigration of settlers demanding land that had slowed down. In the later years of his governorship, since immigration was still free, it would rise exponentially, as those with little money looked to escape Britain and start a new life in a similar way to the "American Dream" in the United States. Between the first and last years of Gipps's governorship, the population of New South Wales nearly doubled, with the total population nearing 200,000 people.

Similar to his liberal predecessor, Gipps had attempted to introduce new policies to accommodate the growing population, namely in education, as the younger population was increasing rapidly in the colonies. However, the councils were opposed to change. There was not much progression, despite the growth of the population. Unemployment was high, and the colony's revenue did not increase from the immigration as it had before.

By 1844, the lack of education in the colony was becoming a real issue since it was holding the colony back from advancing. Although the councils would not allow Gipps to make any changes to the system, he was able to take various surveys and form an education council, which was quite diverse and included men of various religious denominations. According to the Australian National University, it was discovered that "of the estimated 25,676 children between four and fourteen, 7,642 received instruction in public schools, 4,865 in private schools, and the rest no instruction at all." The committee decided that the best course of action would be to introduce the Irish education system, which combined the general learning of a secular school with religious teachings to give children a full education of both religious morals and basic essentials. Almost all were opposed to the idea, including both the Anglican and Catholic churches. However, the Legislative Council decided to pass the Irish education system with one slight adjustment: the children were to have one day off from school to attend church instead of being taught religion in school.

Relations with the Aboriginals

While it is hard to trust reports from 19th-century settlers in Australia when it comes to their relations with the Aboriginals, Gipps was said to be much more humane than the previous governors. During Gipps's governorship, for the first time, Australian Aboriginals were considered to be British subjects. Of course, this came with both positives and negatives. While the Aborigines were to be protected by British laws and could no longer be killed without consequences, the Aboriginal population was expected to attend British schools, be converted, and live on reserved lands. Though the concept of reservations was enacted with the thinking that Aboriginal lands were being protected or "reserved" for the people to keep living their lifestyles, the coastal Aboriginal population was forced to live on reservations in Australia's interior, where they had never lived.

Despite introducing these new laws, many convicts, settlers, and emancipists were far from sympathetic toward the Aboriginals. In

1838, a group of Wirrayaraay, who had lost a good portion of their land, had begun to camp with permission on a landowner's property in Myall Creek in exchange for offering help with labor on the land. Although the Wirrayaraay had shared good relations with the landowner and most of the other workers on the land, which demonstrates that some of the European population had more open views, some of the nearby settlers, convicts, and emancipists were displeased with the agreement. A mixed group of workers on the land that was shared with the Wirrayaraay and nearby Europeans surprised the Aborigines with a violent attack. This led to the death of at least twenty-eight Wirrayaraay people of all ages and genders, even young children. Since Gipps had enacted laws that stated the Aborigines were British subjects, the offenders were put on trial, just as if they had killed European settlers. Despite the massive controversy, they were sentenced to be publicly hanged, which occurred at the end of 1838.

Despite demonstrating that those who committed crimes toward the Aboriginals would be punished, crime continued, and very few offenders were tried following what came to be known as the Myall Creek massacre. The "protectorate," which was the name used to describe the reforms made to protect, convert, and teach the Aborigines, would not end up being successful in almost any way. In 1843, the British government would stop funding missions to convert the Aboriginal population, as they were viewed as a waste of money, especially when the colony was experiencing a financial depression. In 1849, the protectorate program would end altogether, putting an end to all efforts to colonize, convert, or educate the Aboriginal people as if they were British subjects. This is important to note. In almost every other British colony, especially those in the United States and Canada, the colonization and conversion of the Native population was one of the main purposes for settling. Perhaps this is because European settlement happened over a century later in Australia or because conversion was easier in the Americas due to the Native population having developed positive relationships with the Europeans initially.

That being said, despite not undergoing conversion and colonization by the British, the Australian Aboriginals experienced horrendous trauma, fatality rates, and other losses, which was no different than the Native populations of America.

Gipps's Recall

Over the course of Gipps's governorship, his reputation tanked, as did his health. Alongside the councils, the newspapers opposed almost everything that Gipps said, claiming he was not interested in colonial interests but solely in those of the British government, which was a massive insult since the colony was inching toward independence. According to *The Sydney Morning Herald*, "Sir George Gipps has been the worst Governor New South Wales ever had."

In 1846, Gipps's health, which had been gradually plummeting, reached rock bottom. He returned to England in the summer of that year and died around six months later.

Governor Charles Augustus FitzRoy (August 1846 to January 1855)

Before arriving in New South Wales, veteran and Captain Charles Augustus FitzRoy had plenty of political and administrative experience, having been the military secretary and deputy-adjutant general of the Cape of Good Hope. He had served on the House of Commons in England and as the lieutenant governor of both Prince Edward Island and the Leeward Islands. Though the previous governors had similar experience levels before entering the governorship in New South Wales, FitzRoy had something they did not: an aristocratic reputation and connections with the wealthiest and most powerful people in Britain.

Relationship with the Councils

FitzRoy was determined not to repeat the same mistakes as his predecessors and be hated by his Legislative Council. He was adamant about keeping positive relations with the council, even if that meant breaking constitutional laws. An example of this was when the salaries of the councils were supposed to be adjusted. Rather than simply adjust them, at the request of members of the council, FitzRoy sent all of the reports to the members of the council and ultimately determined not to adjust the salaries.

Land Division and Reputation

Similar to his predecessors, FitzRoy had to deal with the issue of squatters, which was essentially replaced the main conflict in the colony at this time. In the Waste Lands Occupation Act of 1846, squatters were given all they had asked for, including tenures, longer leases than Gipps had given, and the right to renewal, amongst other requests. Although some felt that FitzRoy and the secretary of state, Earl Grey, had given up all of the government lands to the squatters, the decision was generally celebrated by the colony. It was seen as a move against the British government, against whom they were growing resentful.

Another act by FitzRoy that was celebrated was when he traveled through a good portion of Australia to determine whether his decision to allow the squatters what they had requested was reasonable. He was the first governor to actually survey and travel through the land to determine his position on a situation. In this case, he discovered that all of the squatters' requests were reasonable.

Within a few months of being in New South Wales, FitzRoy decided to adjust the quitrents system for land that had been put in place by his predecessor. Those who had paid over twenty years of quitrent no longer had to pay, and those who had paid over twenty years received compensation. This was a controversial decision, as it was intensely supported by the colony and completely opposed by the British government. In 1848, Earl Grey was quoted as saying that FitzRoy was "a most incapable Governor of so important a Colony." He believed that FitzRoy no longer cared about being loyal to the Crown or respecting his administrative superiors. To him, FitzRoy only cared about staying on the good side of the population.

Grey and the British government could do little about FitzRoy's disloyalty, as he was beloved by the colony. The recall of the governor might lead to rebellions. That being said, FitzRoy would become slightly controversial amongst the people of the colony after his wife and aide-de-camp died in a carriage accident in 1847. The governor was devastated and even considered returning to England, which left some people to believe he was weak and put women on a pedestal.

Meanwhile, the Port Phillip matter still was on the table: should the settlement still be a part of the New South Wales colony despite being so distant and having different beliefs? After many debates, which essentially destroyed the relationship between Governor FitzRoy and his secretary of state, Earl Grey, the colony of Victoria was created in 1851. The previous year, the Australian Colonies Government Act in 1850 had been passed, which brought representative governments to Tasmania and South Australia. During the course of the debates, FitzRoy used the press as a weapon to destroy Earl Grey's reputation by publishing all of the plans Earl Grey had suggested. FitzRoy knew these would be controversial amongst the population. Even after debating for years, FitzRoy's reputation remained intact due to this strategic move.

Although FitzRoy had managed to maintain some sort of balance between his British and colonial duties, the British government was determined to send more convicts to Australia, despite the colonial population wanting the transportation of convicts to be stopped completely. In the end, after losing the respect of some of his people, a convict ship arrived in Australia in 1848, recommencing the use of the settlements as penal colonies.

Political Reforms

Despite the fact that FitzRoy was the most beloved governor of New South Wales and its dependencies, the colony truly wanted a representative government, fully elected councils, freedom from Great Britain, and a new constitution. FitzRoy felt blindsided when even the new Colonial Office official, the Duke of Newcastle, wanted more elected members in the colony's administration. A new constitution was drawn up in 1850, which would be amended between 1852 and 1853. It called for the establishment of a representative government in the colony.

Chapter 7 – The Australian Gold Rush to the End of the 19th Century (1850 to 1899)

Although the colony had been changing rapidly since the beginning of the 19th century, discoveries in the late 1840s to early 1850s, during FitzRoy's governorship, would lead to exponential, unprecedented developments for Australia. The colony had known about gold for around a decade before the actual gold rush began. In 1841, gold particles were found; however, the discovery was quieted as the governor at the time, George Gipps, worried that the convicts and even the free population would become cut-throat with gold so near. In 1848, gold was discovered again by William Tipple Smith, and he was credited with the first discovery of gold in the colony. After hearing reports of the events occurring in the California gold rush, FitzRoy persuaded his superiors to send a geologist, Samuel Stutchbury, to the colony. In 1849, the discovery of gold was formally announced to the colony, as was the invitation to sell any found gold to the government. Over the following years, gold would be discovered in many of the colonies, including New South Wales, Tasmania, and Victoria.

While gold had already been discovered, the gold rush itself is often credited to have begun after the findings of Edward Hargraves were published in Australian newspapers. Hargraves, who had failed to make profits during the California gold rush, arrived in Ophir, Australia, in 1851 and promptly began digging with John Lister, William Tom, and James Tom. Together, the group found gold, which was brought to Samuel Stutchbury. The group was paid £10,000 by the government for their findings, which Hargraves kept for himself. This was the official beginning of the gold rush, as settlers flooded the confirmed gold deposit in Ophir.

The Governor's Response to the Gold Rush

Although the British colonies had managed to be economically successful and drive great profits for Great Britain, nothing to the degree of a gold rush had ever occurred in a British colony. The situation was made even more complicated by the fact that the colonists were beginning to drift away from their British roots and were heading toward a more independent society. No laws, policies, or systems were in place for a gold rush on colonial lands, so FitzRoy depended heavily on the Executive Council. Promptly, FitzRoy introduced a licensing system, which required all miners to pay 30 shillings a month, hoping that this would help keep the mines orderly and safe, unlike those in California. This licensing fee was necessary since the colonial government was still in debt after their economic crisis. Also, government services and establishments were necessary for the rapidly growing population and expanding settlements. This fee was beneficial for the colonial economy; however, it took a strain on the miners themselves. Furthermore, as required, the colonial government ceded its power in the situation to the British government, which had the ultimate say on all decisions.

Immigration

Although all elements of Australian culture changed due to the gold rush, the most significant changes were debatably those in immigration and the population of the colonies. When gold was discovered, immigration boomed, and the population growth followed the discoveries of gold, which would continue to occur throughout Australia over the course of the second half of the 19th century. From 1851, when the gold rush truly began taking place in Australia, to 1871, when it finally began slowing down, the colony would increase from 430,000 people to 1,700,000. The population of Australia was displaced since colonists emigrated to wherever the gold was. Immigrants came from all over the world; however, most came from European countries and China. By 1855, there were tens of thousands of Chinese miners in Victoria alone. Yet, the Chinese and other non-European miners would receive worse treatment in all aspects of life, from harsher punishment for crimes to lesser payments for gold findings.

Some people traveled to Australia just to see what it was about. Suddenly, there was interest in the British colonies, which had previously only attracted potential landowners. The immigrants brought their own concepts and beliefs, and in September of 1850, the University of Sydney was formed, which attracted young intellectuals.

The Eureka Stockade

After a few years of the Australian gold rush, miners began meeting to discuss their opinions on the mining conditions and the systems that were in place. Most of the miners were opinionated, especially about the high licensing fee, and many of the miners had experience in rebelling and communicating with the government. The new immigrants brought stories of rebellions and political fights with them, which inspired the miners to form their own gatherings. While the meeting started off small, the number of dissatisfied miners grew tenfold by 1853 when miners claimed corrupt police officers began running regular license payment checks in which they would use illegal methods to extort money from the diggers.

On October 6th, 1854, gold miner James Scobie was killed in Ballarat, Victoria, at the Eureka Hotel in what other miners claimed was an incident involving extortion with the hotel's owner, James Bentley. Bentley was acquitted of the charges, but the gold miners felt that some court members had been deceitful since they were known to have financial relationships with Bentley. Over five thousand people met at a miners' gathering to discuss the case, and it was determined that justice had not been served. To ensure Bentley received proper punishment, the group decided to do so themselves and set the Eureka Hotel on fire. Many of the miners were swiftly arrested, and representatives for the miners requested that those arrested be freed.

One hundred fifty soldiers were sent to Ballarat, Victoria, to help control the miners, which only intensified their dissatisfaction. The miners' organization created a Eureka flag, and the flag was hoisted on display for the colonial police and soldiers on November 29th, 1854. The conflicts intensified as the police conducted license searches, which led the miners in the area to a timber stockade to protect themselves. More police and soldiers were called in to destroy the stockade, and on December 3rd, this was accomplished at the expense of over one hundred arrests and the lives of twenty-two miners and six soldiers.

After the leaders of the rebellion were released, debates resumed on how to proceed. Finally, in March 1855, the colonial government decided to get rid of many of the aggressive, crooked police in the gold mines and, most importantly, of the licensing fee for gold miners. Furthermore, eight elected miners were added to the Legislative Council in Victoria. Although no other gold miner rebellion would be as deadly or intense as the Eureka rebellion, similar revolts were occurring all over Australia during the gold rush. Gradually, miners began to earn rights for not only themselves but also the entire colonial population. The gold miner rebellions would lead the colony toward an independent future.

That being said, the colonies still had a way to go before becoming independent, as most of the settlements were quite divided politically between those who profited and those who suffered from the colonial system.

Governor William Thomas Denison (January 1855 to January 1861)

At the end of Charles FitzRoy's term, at the beginning of 1855, he was recalled and replaced with William Thomas Denison, who had been serving as lieutenant governor in Tasmania. There, he displayed his extreme beliefs about the punishment of convicts. Denison took over many of FitzRoy's unresolved conflicts, as well as some new issues plaguing Australia, such as the Crimean War. The Crimean War was being fought in the Crimean Peninsula between Russia on one side and France, the Ottoman Empire, and Britain on the other. Britain's involvement meant that its colonies in Australia were involved as well. Denison helped to construct some of Australia's first military forts and strengthen the colonies' militaries.

Political Reforms

In Australia, the boost in immigration from the gold rush had brought immigrants with liberal opinions, including British immigrants who had participated in the Chartist movement for working-class representation. In Australia, the population began demanding universal male suffrage or, at the very least, allowing all men to vote, meaning land ownership would no longer be a requirement. Furthermore, the movement demanded the use of a secret ballot, which, as the name implies, is anonymous voting that would allow voters to cast their vote free from intimidation and threats.

After many debates and strong opposition from the "exclusives," the Australian Chartists' demands were met. The Electoral Act was passed in 1856 in Victoria, Tasmania, and South Australia. New South Wales would introduce male suffrage in 1858. The government would also separate into a bicameral system, which refers to a parliament that is divided into two; in the case of Australia, it was divided into an entirely elected Legislative Assembly and a nominated Legislative Council. Meanwhile, in South Australia, a new voting system was created, which became known as the Australian ballot, where voters marked an "X" for the candidate they wanted to elect rather than crossing out the names of those they did not choose. This system would later be introduced in Britain and the United States.

Although there had always been political debates, during Denison's governorship, true political divisions within the populace became apparent, likely due to the new social involvement in politics. The liberals focused on land ownership, mostly removing some of the squatters' power and improving working conditions. One of their greater successes in the latter cause was introducing reduced working days; eight-hour shifts were now required, which was a stark difference from the no time limits that had been in place before.

Meanwhile, the wealthy citizens looked to reduce their taxes, increase their profits, and reduce the power of the working class, specifically that of the non-white immigrants, whose population was growing. Both sides also focused on reforming public services, such as education, which led Australia to enforce primary schooling throughout the colonies.

Colonial Reforms between the 1860s and the End of the 19th Century

During Denison's governorship, the colonies in Australia were Victoria, New South Wales, Queensland, South Australia, Tasmania, and Western Australia, which were all essentially acting independently from each other, despite all experiencing similar reforms at once. Every colony had its own social and political reforms and debates. For example, in Victoria, where the wealthy population was still ruled by the liberals, the population was growing, especially in the booming city of Melbourne. Education and tariffs were the main topics of discussion. The working class wanted to introduce taxes that would help improve living and working conditions, while the conservatives opposed these tariffs since they would be paying most of the taxes and gain little from their establishment.

In New South Wales, the people mostly debated over trade and whether it should continue to be protected, which meant high tariffs but secured contracts, or free, which eliminated tariffs and opened trade to everyone. In Queensland, where cattle and sugar farming dominated the economy, debates were held on land expansion and division. South Australia saw similar conversations, and it also had to consider the rights of women, which was becoming a growing demand. Later, in 1863, South Australia adjusted its borders to include the Northern Territory, which had previously been a part of New South Wales. This changed the demographics and topics of interest in the colony.

In Tasmania, democratic practices were being introduced, despite the harsh conditions for workers and the absolutely horrid conditions of the few remaining Aborigines, whose population had been mostly eliminated. Finally, in Western Australia, which was, for most of the 19th century, the slowest developing colony, convicts were at the top of the discussion until the end of their arrival in 1868. A few years earlier, the penal colony on Norfolk Island was closed as well, leading to the deceleration of British convict transports. In the 1890s, development in Western Australia would finally catch up to the rest of Australia's colonies.

Gradual Movement toward Independence

In the mid-1800s, the talk of a federation had grown in Australia, and by the 1870s, the six colonies in Australia began discussing uniting as a federation that would be independent from Great Britain. For some time, New Zealand and Fiji were involved in the conversations. Although it would prove to be unsuccessful and dissolved swiftly, in 1880, representatives from the colonies and their dependencies formed the Australian Natives' Association. The association did not include any actual "Australian Natives." These were white men representing the wants of the settlers who no longer supported Britain's colonial control over Australia.

In 1885, a Federal Council was created that did not include New South Wales, as the colony had decided that gaining independence from Britain and uniting with the other colonies would actually reduce its power. Most of the support for the creation of the federation was actually in Victoria.

In 1889, Sir Henry Parkes of New South Wales spoke of the necessity of a new constitution for the federal government. Parkes convinced the colony of New South Wales to join the council with his iconic speech, which claimed, "The opportunity has arisen for the consideration of this great subject and I believe that the time is at hand...when this thing will be done. Indeed, this great thing will have to be done, and to put it off will only tend to make the difficulties which stand in the way greater." After this speech, Parkes became the leader of the Federal Council. The first convention of the Federal Council was in Sydney in 1891, where the name the "Commonwealth of Australia" was created, as were initial drafts of the new constitution. Further conventions were held between 1897 and 1898 in Adelaide, Sydney, and Melbourne, by which time Parkes had passed and been replaced as leader by Edmund Barton.

Culture during the Second Half of the 19th Century

Meanwhile, as political and social reforms continued to move the colonies toward becoming a federation, the culture in the colonies was diverging from its original British roots, becoming independent and distinct. By the latter half of the 19th century, Australia had developed its own art scene with its own notable artists, from painters to poets to writers.

One of the main themes discussed was Australian independence from Britain. That being said, Australian art at the time was not only inspired by the nationalist movement. Besides current events, Australian artists also touched on the unique Australian landscape and its population, which was made up of tens of thousands of emancipists and hundreds of thousands of people related to convicts.

During this time, Australia began to develop its own stereotypes and characters, separate from those of Great Britain. One example was the "bush worker," who was unique to Australia. He was described as being independent, tough, and somewhat simple-minded, but he was also dependable and willing to help his "mates" whenever asked. Another example of an Australian character was the bushranger, who were simply criminals in the Australian bush who committed very Australian-specific crimes, such as harassing gold miners or the Aboriginal population. The most iconic bushranger was Ned Kelly, who was finally caught and tried in 1880.

Although culture seemed to follow British trends, over the course of the 19th century, simple elements began to divulge. An example of this is in sports. Australia loved football as much as its mother country, yet it gradually began developing its own rules for the game, which is now known as "Australian rules football." The colonies continued to develop culturally, and they became interested in horse racing, attended the Olympics, established their very own stock exchange, constructed a steam train, and created what would become the world's largest mining company in 1885, BHP.

Life for the Aboriginals between 1860 and 1900

With all of the incredible advancements for the colonies culturally, politically, and socially, the land's original people were suffering greatly. While debates were common between liberals and conservatives on the topic of living conditions of the European population, few actually considered or discussed the living conditions of the Aborigines. While some colonies had better conditions and greater sympathy for the Aborigines and the mixed-race population, which was rapidly growing, most settlements maintained racist ideologies that promoted that Aboriginal people needed to be eliminated. This extreme belief was upheld, as the Aboriginal population of Australia decreased from 180,000 in 1861 to 95,000 in 1901.

With all of the reforms taking place in the colonies during this time, missionaries and the colonial administration began losing interest in the Aborigine population and simply sent soldiers to overwhelm and disperse those who rebelled. Although Aboriginal people provided labor services on pastoral farms, their work, which brought about great developments, was rarely mentioned or rewarded.

Chapter 8 – Becoming a Self-governing Nation up to the Second World War (1900 to 1945)

The Commonwealth of Australia

In 1899, referendum bills were sent to New South Wales, South Australia, Tasmania, Queensland, and Victoria, five of the six Australian colonies. At this time, Western Australia was not interested in uniting, as their cities were located so far from the other colonies. Western Australia would join the federation in 1901 after its population boomed. At that point, it agreed with the other colonies to build a train system connecting the distant cities of the west to the rest of Australia. That being said, Western Australia would always be somewhat detached from the federation, and in 1933, it would actually vote on whether to secede from the Commonwealth of Australia.

In the colonies that did participate in the referendum vote, the majority voted to become a federation. Although the Australian colonies (except for Western Australia) had decided to do this, British Parliament still needed to approve the motion for independence. On January 1ˢᵗ, 1901, the Australian colonies would officially become the

Commonwealth of Australia. It was self-governing but still a dominion of Great Britain. In fact, it would not be until 1948 that Australians would be considered Australian citizens and not British citizens.

On the first day of 1901, Australia was publicly and ceremoniously declared a commonwealth, with Edmund Barton, who had been the leader of the Federal Council, as its temporary prime minister. Barton would be officially voted in at the commonwealth's first election on March 29th and 30th, 1901. He would be succeeded in 1903 by Alfred Deakin, who had been his partner in leading the federation movement.

Political Reforms as a Self-Governing Nation

Quickly, the administration began establishing systems and infrastructure that were necessary for a central government to oversee affairs. After some debate, Canberra was chosen as Australia's capital city, where construction of administrative buildings began. The administration was overseen by a parliamentary system made up of the Upper House of Review and the Lower House or the House of Representatives.

Despite becoming self-governing, the administration still had a governor-general, who was assigned by the monarch of Britain. This person oversaw operations in the federation. The power was further divided between the central federal government and the individual states' (formerly known as colonies) governments. As the new system was in transition, for the first decade, the states held much of their previous power. Gradually, the division of state versus federal power took place, dividing up the responsibilities of governing the nation. Although federal laws were introduced that everyone agreed upon, the states in the early years of the federation had differing views on many topics.

The first government was liberal protectionist in nature, and it maintained many liberal beliefs, such as the betterment of working conditions, the imposition of higher tariffs for public services, and the introduction of welfare. That being said, the liberal protectionists were in many ways conservative, at least by today's standards. The Commonwealth of Australia still maintained extreme prejudice toward its non-white civilians, especially as the gold mining immigrants began settling in cities throughout the nation. On December 23rd, 1901, the administration introduced the White Australia Policy, which limited immigration from any foreign country other than those in Europe. For many decades, this policy remained intact, and no immigrants from outside Europe were allowed in the country except on very rare occasions.

Meanwhile, the administration spent the early years of the commonwealth establishing living systems and infrastructure to organize the states. A High Court was established in 1901, which was followed by the creation of the Commonwealth Bank and the development of Australia's military. Most of the Commonwealth of Australia's earliest political conversations were on working conditions, especially after the creation of the Labor Cabinet and the Australian Labor Party. Gradually, unprecedented legislation was introduced that improved the conditions of the working class, such as pensions, which were introduced in 1908, and maternity pay in 1912.

Australia was modernizing quickly during this time. For example, as early as 1902, women could vote in national elections and stand for Australian Parliament, at least in some states. That being said, non-white women and men were not allowed to vote until 1962.

World War I

World War I began on July 28th, 1914, Australia was involved less than a week later when the candidates for prime minister of the commonwealth at the time, Joseph Cook and Andrew Fisher, both swore to support Britain in its military efforts. The development of Australia's military, which had taken place over the course of the past few years, had not only prepared Australians for war strategically, physically, and psychologically, but it also led the population to be excited to participate in the war.

Australia's first significant war efforts began in September of 1914, and their most notable effort was in April of the following year during the Dardanelles campaign in Gallipoli. By the end of World War I, on November 11th, 1918, over 300,000 Australians had participated in military efforts. They suffered around 160,000 injuries and 60,000 deaths. In proportion to the population and budget, Australia contributed some of the most significant efforts to the First World War.

In the years preceding World War I, the commonwealth had been struggling financially, as had most of the world at the time. World War I brought the demand for products from many of Australia's industries, such as vehicles, iron, steel, wool, meat, textiles, and glassmaking. Britain specifically was paying extra for products that would have cost virtually nothing before the war. Overall, Australia would prosper financially from the war; however, the same could not be said about politics at the time. William (Billy) Morris Hughes, who was from the Labor Party and served as the prime minister of Australia for part of World War I, called for Australian conscription. This angered the population but impressed the world, which had previously thought little of Australia's military capabilities. The conscription was not approved during his term as prime minister. Overall, the war represented an important period of change in Australia's politics, which had mostly stayed the same in the decade and a half since the creation of the commonwealth.

Post-World War I

Politics

Although the stress of the war had left many citizens radicalized against the Australian government, this hostility was not shared amongst the veterans who returned home from World War I. Veterans returned home largely in support of the Australian government, and they even went as far as physically punishing the radical citizens, who were believed to be "communists." The Labor Party, which had widespread support and had contributed some of the first prime ministers, started leaning more radical in its anti-war beliefs, which caused them to lose public support. In fact, the prime minister of Australia at the end of the First World War, Billy Hughes, had started off in the Labor Party but was expelled after promoting sending conscripted troops overseas during the war. Hughes would leave the Labor Party to form the National Labor Party, which combined with the Liberal Party to create the Nationalist Party. After Hughes's term ended, Stanley Melbourne Bruce of the Nationalist Party went on to be elected as prime minister.

As mentioned above, politics changed greatly because of the world war. The Labor Party went on to become the Australian Labor Party (ALP), and together with the Country Party, which was supported only by wealthy landowners, the two opposed the Nationalist Party's beliefs and policies. Despite the declining support of the ALP, after Bruce's term ended, he was replaced with an ALP candidate, James Henry Scullin. Division of opinions was common at the house meetings, which included candidates of multiple parties. However, after the war, even the parties themselves had many different opinions. Within the ALP alone, there were conservatives and liberals who disagreed on what the limited government budget should be used for, with some arguing that the commonwealth should pay back its loans to other nations and others saying that it should be used to help the suffering population at home.

Following Scullin's administration, the party controlling Australia would change every term, alternating between the United Australia Party (which was created in 1931), the Country Party, and the Australian Labor Party. The constantly changing parties of the administration and the prime minister demonstrate the political turmoil that had begun in Australia during the First World War. The various administrations attempted to create economic stability by increasing trade with foreign nations. However, the Great Depression was global, and trade was slow. Agreements with other countries and policies to aid the economy internally were established and then aborted. During the post-war years, the administration of Australia had difficulty passing any significant laws, as the parliament was so divided, and people's terms were short-lived.

In response to the lack of reforms for the lower- and working-class, who were suffering the most during the Great Depression, the Australian Communist Party was founded and began to gain some traction. This led Catholics to form the popular Catholic Social Movement, which banded together against communism. Otherwise, politically, in the 1930s, in regards to growing tensions in Europe that would result in World War II, Australia seemed to follow Britain's example and continued to appease Germany and Japan.

The Economy

While Australia's economy had benefited from the demand during World War I, the war did not resolve its economic issues as it had done for other nations around the world. To try and repair the economy, Prime Minister Stanley Bruce attempted to encourage trade deals with and investment from Great Britain while also supporting the creation of Australian companies. However, before long, unemployment rose, as did the cost of living and public debt. Though large corporations and manufacturers recovered, the working class continued to suffer. A loan council and a Council for Scientific and Industrial Research were created to help study and solve the economic and developmental issues in the commonwealth. Despite all of the demand for Australian products during the war, in the post-war period, wool was the only product in high demand.

The economic crisis developed into the Great Depression, where more than a quarter of the population was unemployed. The working-class population was entirely miserable. By the 1930s, the immigration balance had reversed, as more people were leaving the country than immigrating to it.

World War II

Since Australia remained a dominion of Britain, when World War II broke out in 1939, Australia was amongst the first countries to join the Allies. The Commonwealth of Australia promptly introduced required military training, which forced all men over twenty-one to train for at least three months. Conscription was later introduced for the Australian Imperial Force. After the Japanese attacked Pearl Harbor, Australia began warring with Japan, which brought the war closer to home. By 1941, Australia itself was under attack from Japan. Some of the worst conflicts at home were the bombing in northern Australia and the attack on Sydney Harbour.

The war allowed Australia to make new allies, including the United States, which actually came to help Australia defend itself from Japanese attacks. The conflict between Japan and Australia continued to escalate, and both nations had prisoner-of-war camps to detain soldiers. Japan had over ten thousand Australians as prisoners of war, who actually had to help construct railways throughout Asia. Meanwhile, Australia had over twenty prisoner-of-war camps, which held more than twelve thousand prisoners. By the end of the war, it is estimated around sixty-five thousand Australians were injured, and at least thirty thousand were killed.

Aside from all of the violence, the Second World War, like the First World War, brought some good to Australia. Once again, manufacturing boomed as the demand for aircraft, chemicals, and machines grew. Since so many men were away at war, women began filling positions in factories. Before long, families who had been impoverished during the 1930s were prospering. Between the end of World War I and the end of World War II, the commonwealth's GNP (gross national product) almost tripled.

Aboriginal Conditions between the Turn of the Century and World War II

As mentioned throughout this book, much of the reporting on the treatment of Australian Aboriginals by the colonial and federal governments were downplayed and rewritten, making it hard to truly comprehend the atrocities that occurred. In the first years after the creation of the Commonwealth of Australia, the new federal administration focused on assimilating the younger Aboriginal generations. Though this may not sound horrendous, it is estimated that between 1910 and 1970, tens of thousands of Aboriginal children were taken away from their families, put into the Australian adoption system, renamed, and forced to become "Australian." Meanwhile, wars between the Aboriginals and white Australians continued.

Chapter 9 – Australia Post-World War II (1945 to 1980)

Economy

As mentioned in the last chapter, both world wars had incredible effects on the economy of the Commonwealth of Australia. However, unlike the First World War, where the suffering economy was repaired and then went back to being crippled, the positive economic effects lasted after the end of World War II. Although there were still many financial issues that needed addressing during the post-war period, for example, the conditions of the non-male working class, the years after World War II marked a sort of golden financial age for Australia. As immigration to Australia increased, especially after the foreign immigration restrictions were removed in the 1970s, internal spending more than doubled. This helped to restart Australia's economy. External demand increased as well in the post-war years, which led to massive profits and growth in the wool, manufactured goods, electronics, and automobile industries. Although Australia had an extremely rich cultural scene, notably in the arts and sports, since its independence, Australian culture became better known globally after the end of World War II. This was accelerated in 1956 when Melbourne held the Olympic Games, which helped to attract admiration and tourism to the nation, all of which benefited its economy.

The previous American occupation in Australia, which had helped to protect the nation from Japanese threats during the war, would turn out to be beneficial after the war. Australia began trade relations with the United States, which resulted in a boom in exports to the United States, as well as the imports of products that could be made cheaper on American soil. That being said, Australia's relationship with America was not only financial. Slowly, elements of American culture began sneaking their way into Australian society. Some examples of this were in Australian films and music, which was changing due to the American influence. Gradually, film became a massive industry in Australia, as the popularity of both theaters and televisions rose in the post-war years.

Immigration

After World War II, the Australian government decided to facilitate immigration from all over Europe. In 1950, immigration reached its peak, as around 150,000 people immigrated to the commonwealth in one year. Immigration restrictions were slowly eased until finally, the White Australia Policy, which had been introduced in the first year of Australia's independence, ended. In 1945, the population of Australia was 7,391,692; in only five years, the population increased to 8,177,342. By 1970, the population had already reached 12,793,034. Although this mass immigration was overall positive, it did lead to many issues since the country was still extremely prejudiced and, by modern standards, racist in the post-war years.

Politics

Prime Minister John Curtin, who had been quite influential since he led during the entirety of World War II, passed away in July just before the end of the war. He was succeeded by Joseph Benedict Chifley (also known as Ben Chifley), who was also a member of the ALP. In the post-war years, Chifley invested much of his efforts into aiding the growth of the economy and improving working conditions. Gradually, under the prime ministers of the post-war years, the federal government absorbed some of the state powers. Economic changes were also propelled by Chifley's successor, Robert Menzies of the Liberal Party. During his term, public education services grew, as did anti-communist efforts. The Commonwealth of Australia took part in the Cold War, specifically in Korea.

The administration would continue to switch hands. In the 1970s, the Labor Party's Edward Gough Whitlam became the prime minister. He would make great strides for workers, notably by increasing wages and equal pay for women. Whitlam and all of his successors began focusing on creating a "better" Australia, one that would make Australians proud and attract interest from foreigners. During this time, health and education were improved, as were public services and transit systems.

During World War II, Australia had made many foreign relationships. It had been put on the map. Gradually, international affairs became one of the more important aspects of politics. Prime Minister Herbert Vere Evatt, who held the position between 1951 and 1960, actually helped to create the United Nations. Meanwhile, Australia remained on good terms with Great Britain. Despite forging their own distinct identity, Australians enthusiastically welcomed Britain's Queen Elizabeth II in 1954. Over the course of the post-war period, Australia even began to forge new relations with Japan. Though hostilities still existed between the two nations that had caused one another so much harm, the two started reintroducing economic relations. Trade between Australia and Japan restarted in 1949, and within twenty years, Japan received more exports from Australia than the United Kingdom.

Social

The post-war years brought great change socially for Australia, mostly due to the increase in immigration, which rippled through both the economy and politics. Minority struggles and liberal beliefs became important conversations as the debatably radical "new left" grew. This culminated in the creation of the Australian Democrats in 1977, which would remain a minority party. However, it would help to diffuse "radical" democratic concepts and shape the commonwealth's future. Gradually, feminist, environmentalist, and LGBTQ organizations gained momentum and influenced changes that would carry Australia into its modern-day beliefs.

Aboriginals

Although conditions remained difficult for the Aboriginal people of Australia, activism and awareness gained popularity in the years following World War II. This had positive impacts on the Aboriginal population. Between the 1930s and 1980s, the Aboriginal population more than doubled in Australia. Despite being descendants of the first humans in Australia, in 1962, Aboriginals were finally considered to be Australians. Gradually, Aboriginal matters became more important to the government. The Aboriginal Land Rights Act was introduced in 1976, and Aboriginals later began earning royalties from gold mining on their reserved land. In 1973, the National Aboriginal Consultative Committee (now the National Aboriginal Conference) was founded. Slowly, Aboriginals made their way into Australia's cultural awareness, as they became acclaimed artists, athletes, and politicians.

That being said, much of the damage had already been done. As the Aboriginals developed, they changed and lost elements of their culture, as any population does. However, this development was not natural but instead forced by the European colonies. Despite the Aboriginal population being over 170,000 in the 1980s, only around 10,000 Aboriginals actually maintained a "traditional" Aboriginal lifestyle. Though Aboriginals maintained their history through stories and art, by the turn of the century, Aboriginals in Australia were almost completely integrated into European Australian lifestyles.

Chapter 10 – Australia Today (1980 to Today)

Social

Throughout the past few decades, gradual social reforms, specifically in human rights, working conditions, and equality, have transformed Australia into what it is today. Despite not allowing any non-white, non-European immigrants to move to Australia for around half of the 20th century, by the 1980s, foreign immigration had propelled massively. By the early 2000s, around one-third of Australia's non-Aboriginal population was Asian. This boom in immigration forced the government to modernize its opinions on non-white people, drastically speeding up its modernization.

In the year 2000, a survey done by the United Nations rated Australia in the top five for quality of life in the world. After cultural developments in arts and sports, such as Sydney hosting the Olympic Games, which combined the two, Australia made its way into the global eye. That being said, Australia was not and continues to not be a perfect place. Though Australia is considered to be one of the best places to live, natural disasters and desolation often occur. While natural disasters have always been a part of Australia's climate, the effects are much more disastrous now since it has become more populous. In 2009, bushfires spread across the landmass, killing over one hundred people in Victoria. The deadliest of these incidents during this time was in Melbourne, and it is known as Black Saturday. Bushfires have continued to plague Australia, and in 2019 and 2020, wildfires, combined with extreme heat, drought, wind, and lightning, burned almost eighteen million acres of land across the continent. Bushfires are not the only natural occurrence desolating areas either. In 2021, Australia experienced disastrous rainfall, cyclones, and flooding, which caused nearly twenty thousand people to be displaced from their homes.

Politics

Since the creation of the commonwealth, Australia has been divided politically. However, this division only grew in the years following World War II and has continued to intensify in the past forty years. New political movements are being formed constantly, as the population searches for leaders who will represent their beliefs. One example of a new political movement is that of the One Nation Movement of the 1990s. Formed by Pauline Hanson, One Nation was a right-wing, nationalist political movement that celebrated the Anglo-Celtic ethnicity and condemned multiculturalism in Australia. Despite being extreme, One Nation gained some serious traction in the 1990s, and Hanson even received a seat in Parliament.

Since 1968, political power has constantly switched between the Labor and the Liberal parties of Australia, with neither one usually gaining the majority in Parliament. While both parties are left-leaning, they differ in enough ways to continue to compete rather than merge. This meant that every time the administration switched, policies switched. For decades, Australia's laws were slightly unstable since they were introduced and aborted with every new prime minister. Taxes would be introduced for climate action, then removed, then reintroduced. However, since 2013, Australia has been in the hands of the Liberal Party.

Despite Australia being divided politically, the country is comparatively liberal, and the conservative-leaning party is still more liberal than in most other countries. This is demonstrated in the fact that since the 1960s, the country has elected either one of the two left-leaning parties into office. In 2010, Australia's first female prime minister, Julia Gillard, was elected into office. In 2017, same-sex marriage was introduced.

To this day, Australia remains a part of the British monarchy, despite the introduction of the Australia Act in 1986, which released the former colony of its dominionship. In the 1990s, the administration considered updating the constitution in order to completely cut the ties that kept Australia connected to Great Britain and officially become a republic. A referendum was held in 1999, and the people voted on whether they would want the monarch and governor-general to be replaced by a president. Despite being a distinct nation from Britain with its own strong nationalism, many Australians still feel connected to their monarchical roots, and the majority voted not to alter the constitution.

Aboriginals

A couple of decades ago, conditions were getting better for the Aboriginal people, as the situation had improved with indigenous land-rights claims. That being said, the Australian administration still refused to acknowledge all the wrongdoing they had done to the Aboriginal population. History books were only beginning to teach that Aboriginals inhabited the land before British settlement. Finally, in the 2010s, Australia's government began to apologize for the government's previous actions. By the turn of the century, around 500,000 Australians were reported to be partially Aboriginal.

Conclusion

Today, Australia is considered to be one of the best nations to live in, yet for most of history, life was not so easy. The first people struggled to survive on the land, but through thousands of years of development, they managed to thrive and form complex systems. Although the Europeans believed it was uninhabitable, after the loss of the United States, Britain decided to send its convicts to Australia; thus, the first settlement was almost entirely made up of convicts and their jailers.

The early years of the settlement were difficult since survival was difficult. Food and water were hard to come by, and working conditions were severe for the convicts. Yet, after some time, convict punishment lightened, exploration led to richer lands that were better for agriculture, and infrastructure was established to make life more comfortable. Convicts in Australia generally served short sentences, as those who had committed serious crimes were simply killed.

Although immigrants were not interested in living in the penal colony at first, land grants gained interest. Soon, the European population of Australia was no longer mostly convicts but emancipists and free settlers. Life was initially difficult for the ex-convicts, who were looked down upon by the free settlers. Gradually, though, emancipists made their way up the social ladder and became equals to the free settlers. During the gold rush, Australians began to develop their own unique culture, opinions, and systems that were distinctly different from Britain, and eventually, the colonies united to become states of the Commonwealth of Australia.

Overall, Australia's history is one of survival, regardless of the harsh, arid landmass that the population chose to live on. However, amongst the stories of survival, it is necessary to acknowledge that progression rarely comes without any expense. Throughout Australia's history, its growth into a successful, affluent, self-governing, modern, and liberal society came at the expense of the Aboriginal population, who inhabited the land first. For most of history, the suffering that was caused to the territory's first people was disregarded and hidden. Until recently, Australians had little understanding of the true scope of their history. However, history is being uncovered daily, and Australians are gradually learning about their land's origins, which is necessary to comprehend exactly how lucky the current population is.

Here's another book by Captivating History that you might like

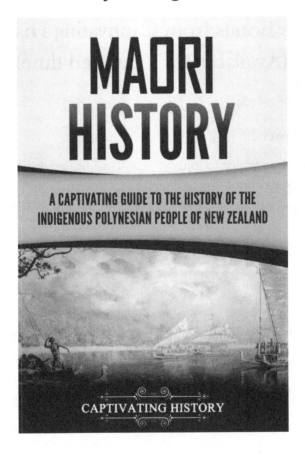

Free Bonus from Captivating History
(Available for a Limited time)

Hi History Lovers!

Now you have a chance to join our exclusive history list so you can get your first history ebook for free as well as discounts and a potential to get more history books for free! Simply visit the link below to join.

Captivatinghistory.com/ebook

Also, make sure to follow us on Facebook, Twitter and Youtube by searching for Captivating History.

Bibliography

Auchmuty, J. J. "Hunter, John (1737–1821)." *Biography - John Hunter*, 1 Jan. 1966,

https://adb.anu.edu.au/biography/hunter-john-2213

Australian Dictionary of Biography, National Centre of Biography. "Darling, Sir Ralph (1772–1858)." *Australian National University*, 1 Jan. 1966,

https://adb.anu.edu.au/biography/darling-sir-ralph-1956

Australian Dictionary of Biography. "Bourke, Sir Richard (1777–1855)." *Biography - Sir Richard Bourke*, 1 Jan. 1966, https://adb.anu.edu.au/biography/bourke-sir-richard-1806

Australian War Memorial. "Australians in World War II." *Australian War Memorial, London*, 2022, https://www.awmlondon.gov.au/australians-in-wwii

Australian War Memorial. "First World War 1914–18." *Australian War Memorial*, 2022, https://www.awm.gov.au/articles/atwar/first-world-war

Australians Together. "Busting the Myth of Peaceful Settlement." *Australians Together*, 2022, https://australianstogether.org.au/discover/australian-history/busting-the-myth-of-peaceful-settlement

Australians Together. "Colonisation Dispossession, Disease and Direct Conflict." *Australians Together*, 2022, https://australianstogether.org.au/discover/australian-history/colonisation

BBC. "Australia Profile -Timeline." *BBC News*, BBC, 7 Jan. 2020, https://www.bbc.com/news/world-asia-15675556

Black, David W. "Shell Middens." *The Canadian Encyclopedia*, 13 June 2019, https://www.thecanadianencyclopedia.ca/en/article/shell-middens

Britannica, The Editors of Encyclopedia. "Arthur Phillip." *Encyclopedia Britannica*, Encyclopedia Britannica, Inc., 7 Oct. 2021, https://www.britannica.com/biography/Arthur-Phillip

britannica, The Editors of Encyclopedia. "Botany Bay." *Encyclopedia Britannica*, Encyclopedia Britannica, Inc., 19 Dec. 2017, https://www.britannica.com/place/Botany-Bay

Britannica, The Editors of Encyclopedia. "Bushranger." *Encyclopedia Britannica*, Encyclopedia Britannica, Inc., 29 Oct. 2020, https://www.britannica.com/topic/bushranger

Britannica, The Editors of Encyclopedia. "Dirck Hartog." *Encyclopedia Britannica*, Encyclopedia Britannica, Inc., 27 May 2019, https://www.britannica.com/biography/Dirck-Hartog

Britannica, The Editors of Encyclopedia. "George Bass." *Encyclopedia Britannica*, Encyclopedia Britannica, Inc., Jan. 2022, https://www.britannica.com/biography/George-Bass

Britannica, The Editors of Encyclopedia. "Lachlan Macquarie." *Encyclopedia Britannica*, Encyclopedia Britannica, Inc., Jan. 2022, https://www.britannica.com/biography/Lachlan-Macquarie

Britannica, The Editors of Encyclopedia. "Lachlan Macquarie." *Encyclopedia Britannica*, Encyclopedia Britannica, Inc., Jan. 2022, https://www.britannica.com/biography/Lachlan-Macquarie

Britannica, The Editors of Encyclopedia. "Madjedbebe." *Encyclopedia Britannica*, Encyclopedia Britannica, Inc., 11 Aug. 2019,

https://www.britannica.com/place/Madjedbebe

Britannica, The Editors of Encyclopedia. "Matthew Flinders." *Encyclopedia Britannica*, Encyclopedia Britannica, Inc., 2022, https://www.britannica.com/biography/Matthew-Flinders

Britannica, The Editors of Encyclopedia. "Nauwalabila I." *Encyclopedia Britannica*, Encyclopedia Britannica, Inc., 20 Oct. 2020,

https://www.britannica.com/place/Nauwalabila-I

Britannica, The Editors of Encyclopedia. "Sahul Shelf." *Encyclopedia Britannica*, Encyclopedia Britannica, Inc., 9 Aug. 2007, https://www.britannica.com/place/Sahul-Shelf

Britannica, The Editors of Encyclopedia. "Sir Thomas Makdougall Brisbane, Baronet." *Encyclopedia Britannica*, Encyclopedia Britannica, Inc., Jan. 2022,

https://www.britannica.com/biography/Sir-Thomas-Makdougall-Brisbane-Baronet

Britannica, The Editors of Encyclopedia. "Stanley Melbourne Bruce." *Encyclopedia Britannica*, Encyclopedia Britannica, Inc., 1 Sept. 2021,

https://www.britannica.com/biography/Stanley-Melbourne-Bruce

Britannica, The Editors of Encyclopedia. "Sunda Shelf." *Encyclopedia Britannica*, Encyclopedia Britannica, Inc., 12 Apr. 2016, https://www.britannica.com/place/Sunda-Shelf

Britannica, The Editors of Encyclopedia. "W.C. Wentworth." *Encyclopedia Britannica*, Encyclopedia Britannica, Inc., 2022, https://www.britannica.com/biography/W-C-Wentworth

Britannica, The Editors of Encyclopedia. "William Dampier." *Encyclopedia Britannica*, Encyclopedia Britannica, Inc., 2022, https://www.britannica.com/biography/William-Dampier

Crockett, Gary. "Australian Convict Sites." *Sydney Living Museums*, 22 Jan. 2014, https://sydneylivingmuseums.com.au/convict-sydney/australian-convict-sites-world-heritage

Currey, C. H. "Denison, Sir William Thomas (1804–1871)." *Biography - Sir William Thomas Denison*, Australian Dictionary of Biography, 1 Jan. 1972,

https://adb.anu.edu.au/biography/denison-sir-william-thomas-3394

Deadly Story. "Frontier Wars." *Deadly Story*, 2022,

https://www.deadlystory.com/page/culture/history/Frontier_wars

Dening, Greg. "William Bligh." *Encyclopedia Britannica*, Encyclopedia Britannica, Inc., 3 Dec. 2021, https://www.britannica.com/biography/William-Bligh

Dorey, Fran. "When Did Modern Humans Get to Australia?" *The Australian Museum*, 12 Sept. 2021, https://australian.museum/learn/science/human-evolution/the-spread-of-people-to-australia

Ducksters. "Australia History and Timeline Overview." *Ducksters, Technological Solutions, Inc. (TSI)*, 2022,

https://www.ducksters.com/geography/country/australia_history_timeline.php

Heydon, J. D. "Brisbane, Sir Thomas Makdougall (1773–1860)." *Biography - Sir Thomas Makdougall Brisbane*, 1 Jan. 1966, https://adb.anu.edu.au/biography/brisbane-sir-thomas-makdougall-1827

Hiscocks, Richard. "Philip Gidley King." *More than Nelson*, 2018, https://morethannelson.com/officer/philip-gidley-king

Jeans, D. N., Brown, Nicholas and Fletcher, Brian Hinton. "New South Wales."

Encyclopedia Britannica, Encyclopedia Britannica, Inc., 19 Oct. 2021, https://www.britannica.com/place/New-South-Wales

Khan Academy. "Motivation for European Conquest of the New World." *Khan Academy*, Khan Academy, 2022, https://www.khanacademy.org/humanities/us-history/precontact-and-early-colonial-era/old-and-new-worlds-collide/a/motivations-for-conquest-of-the-new-world

Kästle, Klaus. "History of Australia." *History of Australia - Nations Online Project*, 2017, https://www.nationsonline.org/oneworld/History/Australia-history.htm

andini, Posted by David. "Formation of the Australian States. 1788 – 1989." *The Riverina State*, 11 Oct. 2017, https://theriverinastate.com.au/2017/10/11/evolution-of-australian-states

Linklater, Scott. "Understanding Aboriginal Dreaming and the Dreamtime." *Artlandish Aboriginal Art*, 2022, https://www.aboriginal-art-australia.com/aboriginal-art-library/understanding-aboriginal-dreaming-and-the-dreamtime

Macro Trends. "Australia Population 1950-2022." *MacroTrends*, 2022, https://www.macrotrends.net/countries/AUS/australia/population

McCulloch, Samuel Clyde. "Gipps, Sir George (1791–1847)." *Biography - Sir George Gipps*, Australian Dictionary of Biography, 1 Jan. 1966, https://adb.anu.edu.au/biography/gipps-sir-george-2098

National Library of Australia. "How Was Australia Named?" *National Library of Australia*, 2022, https://www.nla.gov.au/faq/how-was-australia-named

National Library of Australia. "Who Was the First European to Land on Australia?" *National Library of Australia*, 2022, https://www.nla.gov.au/faq/who-was-the-first-european-to-land-on-australia

National Museum of Australia. "Opening up the Continent." *Europeans Cross the Blue Mountains | Australia's Defining Moments Digital Classroom | National Museum of Australia,* 2022, https://digital-classroom.nma.gov.au/defining-moments/europeans-cross-blue-mountains

Parliament of New South Wales. "1788 To 1810 - Early European Settlement." *Parliament of New South Wales,* 2022, https://www.parliament.nsw.gov.au/about/Pages/1788-to-1810-Early-European-Settlement.aspx

Parliament of New South Wales. "1810 To 1821 - Governor Lachlan Macquarie." *Parliament of New South Wales,* 2022, https://www.parliament.nsw.gov.au/about/Pages/1810-to-1821-Governor-Lachlan-Macquarie.aspx

Persse, Michael. "Wentworth, William Charles (1790–1872)." *Biography - William Charles Wentworth,* 1 Jan. 1967, https://adb.anu.edu.au/biography/wentworth-william-charles-2782

Persse, Michael. "Wentworth, William Charles (1790–1872)." *Biography - William Charles Wentworth,* Australian Dictionary of Biography, 1 Jan. 1967

https://adb.anu.edu.au/biography/wentworth-william-charles-2782

Rule of Law Education Centre. "Governor John Hunter." *Rule of Law Education Centre,* 2022, https://www.ruleoflaw.org.au/wp-content/uploads/Governor-John-Hunter.pdf

Rule of Law Education Centre. "Governor William Bligh." *Rule of Law Education Centre,* 2022, https://www.ruleoflaw.org.au/wp-content/uploads/Governor-William-Bligh.pdf

Smith, Tom. "Why Great Britain Sent Its Prisoners to Australia." *Culture Trip,* The Culture Trip, 13 Aug. 2018, https://theculturetrip.com/pacific/australia/articles/why-great-britain-sent-its-prisoners-to-australia

Sood, Amy. "Scientists Confirm Discovery of Australia's Largest Dinosaur." *CNN*, Cable News Network, 8 June 2021, https://www.cnn.com/2021/06/08/australia/australia-dinosaur-largest-discovery-intl-hnk-scn/index.html

St. Fleur, Nicholas. "Humans First Arrived in Australia 65,000 Years Ago, Study Suggests." *The New York Times*, The New York Times, 19 July 2017,

https://www.nytimes.com/2017/07/19/science/humans-reached-australia-aboriginal-65000-years.html

Sydney Living Museums. "Sir Ralph Darling." *Sydney Living Museums*, 1 Sept. 2017, https://sydneylivingmuseums.com.au/convict-sydney/sir-ralph-darling

Tonkinson, Robert and Berndt, Ronald M. "Australian Aboriginal Peoples." *Encyclopedia Britannica*, Encyclopedia Britannica, Inc., 19 Apr. 2018,

https://www.britannica.com/topic/Australian-Aboriginal

Tourism Australia. "Plan Your Trip to Australia." *Visit Australia - Travel & Tour Information - Tourism Australia*, 2022,

https://www.australia.com/en-ca/facts-and-planning/history-of-australia.html

Twidale, Charles Rowland, Ride, W. D. L., Rickard, John David, Veevers, John J., Roe, Michael, Powell, Joseph Michael and Lange, Robert Terence. "Australia." *Encyclopedia Britannica*, Encyclopedia Britannica, Inc., 2022,

https://www.britannica.com/place/Australia

Villiers, Alan John. "James Cook." *Encyclopedia Britannica*, Encyclopedia Britannica, Inc., 2022, https://www.britannica.com/biography/James-Cook

Wallis, Helen Margaret. "Abel Tasman." *Encyclopedia Britannica*, Encyclopedia Britannica, Inc., 24 Feb. 2021, https://www.britannica.com/biography/Abel-Tasman

Ward, John M. "Fitzroy, Sir Charles Augustus (1796–1858)." *Biography - Sir Charles Augustus FitzRoy*, Australian Dictionary of Biography, 1 Jan. 1966,

https://adb.anu.edu.au/biography/fitzroy-sir-charles-augustus-2049

Welch, David M. "Aboriginal Culture - Housing and Shelters." *Aboriginal Culture AU*, Aboriginal Culture AU, 2022, https://www.aboriginalculture.com.au/housing-and-shelters

Welch, David M. "Aboriginal Culture - Social Organisation." *Aboriginal Culture Au*, Aboriginal Culture Au, 2022, https://www.aboriginalculture.com.au/social-organisation

Welch, David M. "Aboriginal Culture - Bush Foods." *Aboriginal Culture AU*, Aboriginal Culture AU, 2022, https://www.aboriginalculture.com.au/bush-foods

Welch, David M. "Aboriginal Culture - Ceremonial Life." *Aboriginal Culture AU*, Aboriginal Culture AU, 2022, https://www.aboriginalculture.com.au/ceremonial-life

Welch, David M. "Aboriginal Culture - Fishing Methods." *Aboriginal Culture AU*, Aboriginal Culture AU, 2022, https://www.aboriginalculture.com.au/fishing-methods

Welch, David M. "Aboriginal Culture - Regional Variations." *Aboriginal Culture AU*, Aboriginal Culture AU, 2022, https://www.aboriginalculture.com.au/regional-variations

Made in the USA
Las Vegas, NV
10 December 2023

82465693R00075